HERBS, FLAVOURS AND SPICES

TO MY MOTHER

who distilled her infinite wisdom into several pure component parts so that one of these should arouse within me an unquenchable thirst for useful knowledge of fragrance and the delicate art of seasoning with spices and herbs. Only after this knowledge was acquired did she help me with my charts, which have led to so many delicious and fascinating flavours.

Contents

7

Contents

Contents

The Setting

Go, little book, and wish to all
Flowers in the garden, meat in the hall,
A bin of wine, a spice of wit,
A house with lawn enclosing it,
A living river by the door,
A nightingale in the sycamore!

ROBERT LOUIS STEVENSON

Mankind has been drawn by the exotic lure of spices and herbs since before recorded history. No other commodities of commerce have had such an all-encompassing place in history, adventure, legend, and lore. In ancient times they stirred the imagination of kings and ambitious adventurers to seek sea routes to Asia in an effort to reach the riches that were waiting for a taker. Thus, the New World was found.

The great writers down through the ages have found the mysteries of spices and herbs to be delightful subjects. Theophrastus of Greece wrote *On the History of Plants* and *On the Causes of Plants*. Dioscorides of Greece was next to contribute to the field of horticulture. Galen, also of Greece, was a physician who wrote of medicinal plants and invented the formula for cold creams. Pliny, a Roman, found time to study and write about the virtues of frail and perishable plants. William Turner wrote the first English herbal in 1539 and John Gerard from London spent more than thirty-six years in the 17th century in growing, classifying, and writing about plants from all parts of the world. John Parkinson, also from London, made a great contribution through his *Theatre of Plants*, published in 1640.

Collinson of London corresponded with Custis of Williamsburg and Bartram of Philadelphia, who were the earliest American writers on botany. Their love of horticulture taught the meaning and necessity of plant exchange between countries and individuals.

The Setting

The beautiful *Song of Solomon* and the nostalgic writings of Shakespeare are filled with references to sweet-smelling spices and herbs that pervade many gardens to this day.

The dreams and ideals of the first settlers in America were expressed through their gardens and terraced walks, in which their heritage and vistas of the past were evident.

My father, Edgar W. Smith, was a timber surveyor and contractor. As a result, it was my good fortune to grow up with nature. When he was growing up the kitchen herb garden was a must for every family, and he taught me how to plant my first herb garden on his plantation. It was planted in a wheel from one of his wagons. An interest in having my own garden has been with me since childhood.

After joining a garden club I became interested in collecting data on spices and herbs. The material was useful on garden club and television programmes and in garden therapy work: sweet-scented herb gardens enriched the lives of the house-bound, the aged, and the blind.

Practically all authorities agree that retired people become such enthusiastic gardeners because of the future outlook, for 'Gardening is a constant succession of new beginnings.' The 'Pleasure Garden' for fragrance and flavour has become one of the most popular of their planting and growing projects.

This is not a technical book. It is a book of stories built on a foundation of history and an endless number of books. The compiled material took book form so that the history, romance, adventure, legend and lore of fragrance, flavour, and beauty—our heritage of spices and herbs—might be shared with many, many others.

E. S. H.

PART ONE

Assembly of the Herbs

1. Dedication of Gerard's Herball

'To THE RIGHT HONORABLE HIS SINGULAR GOOD LORD AND MASTER, Sir William Cecil Knight, BARON OF Burghly, Master of the Courts of Wards and Liveries, Chancelloer of the Universities of Cambridge, Knight of the most noble Order of the Garter, one of the Lords of her Majesties most honorable Privy Councill, and Lord high Treasure of England.

'Among the manifold creatures of God (right Honorable, and singular good Lord) that have all in all ages diversely entertained many excellent wits, and drawn them to contemplation of the divine wisdome, none have provoked mans studies more, or satisfied their desires so much as plants have done, and that upon just and worthy causes: for if delight may provoke mens labor, what greater delight is there than to behold the earth apparelled with plants, as with a robe of embroidered worke, set with Orient pearles and garnished with great diversities of rare and costly jewels? If this varietie and perfection of colours may affect the eie, it is such in herbs and floures, that no Apelles, no Zevxis ever could by any art expresse the like: if odours or if taste may worke satisfaction, they are both so soveraigne in plants, and so comfortable that no confection of the Apothecaries can equall their excellent vertue. But these delights are in the outward senses: the principal delight is in the mind, singularly enriched with the knowledge of these visible things, setting forth to us the invisible wisdome and admirable work-manship of Almighty God. The delight is great, but the use is greater, and joyned often with necessitie. In the first ages of the world they were the ordinary meate of men, and have continued ever since of necessary use both for meates to maintaine life, and for medicine to recover health. The hidden vertue of them is such, that (as Pliny noteth) the very bruit beasts have found it out: and (which is another use that he observes) from thence the Dyars took the beginning of their Art.

15

'Furthermore, the necessary use of those fruits of the earth doth plainly appeare by the great charge and care of almost all men in planting & maintaining of gardens, not as ornaments onely, but as a necessarie provision also to their houses.

'And here besides the fruit, to speake againe in a word of delight, gardens, especialy such as your Honor hath, furnished with many rare Simples, do singularly delight, when in them a man doth behold a flourishing shew of Summer beauties in the midst of Winter forces, and a goodly Spring of floures, when abroad a leafe is not to be seene. Besides these and other causes, there are many examples of those that have honoured this Science: for to passe by a multitude of the Philosophers, it may please your Honor to call to remembrance that which you know of some noble Princes, that have joyned this study with their most important matters of state: Mithridates the great was famous for his knowledge herein, as Plutarch noteth. Evax also King of Arabia, the happy garden of the world for principall Simples, wrot of this argument, as Pliny sheweth. Dioclesian likewise, might have had this praise, had he not drowned all his honour in the bloud of his persecution. To conclude this point, the example of Solomon is before the rest, and greater, whose wisdom and knowledge was such, that hee was able to set out the nature of all plants from the highest Cedar to the lowest Mosse. But my good Lord, that which sometime was the study of great Phylosophers and mightie Princes, is now neglected, except it be of some few, whose spirit and wisdome hath carried them among other parts of wisdome and counsell, to care and studies of special herbs, both for the furnishing of their gardens, and furtherance of their knowledge: among whom I may justly affirme and publish your Honor to be one, being my self one of your servants, and long time witnesse thereof: for under your Lordship I have served, and that way emploied my principall study and almost all my time, now by the space of twenty yeares. To the large and singular furniture of this noble Island I have added from forreine places all varieties of herbs and flowers that I might any way obtaine, I have laboured with the soile to make it fit for plants, that they might delight in the soile, that so they might live and prosper under our clymat, as in their native and proper countrey: what my sucesse hath beene, and what my furniture is, I leave to the report of they that have seen your Lordships gardens, and the little plot of myne owne especiall care and husbandry. But because gardens are private, and many times finding an ignorant or negligent successor, come soone to ruine, there be that have sollicited me, first by my pen, and after by the press to make my labors common, and to free them from the danger wherunto a garden is subject: wherein when I was overcome, and brought this History or report of nature of Plants to a just volume, and made it (as the Reader may by comparison see) richer than former Herbals, I found it no question unto whom I might dedicate my labors; for considering your good Lordship, I found none of whose favour and goodness I might sooner presume, seeing I have found you ever my very good Lord and Master. Againe, considering my duty and your Honors merits, to whom may I better recommend my Labors, than to him unto whom I owe my selfe, and all that I am able in your service or devotion to performe? Therefore under hope of your Honorable and acustomed favor I present this Herball to your Lordships protection; and not as an exquisite Worke (for I know my Meannesse) but as the greatest gift and chiefest argument of duty that my labour and service can affoord: wherof if there be no other fruit, yet this is of some use, that I have ministred Matter for men of riper wits and deeper judgements to polish, and to adde to my large additions where anything is defective, that in time the Worke may be perfect. Thus I humbly take my leave, beseeching God to grant to you many daies to live to his glory, to support of this State under her Majestie our dread Soveraigne, and that with great increase of honor in this world, and all fulness of glory in the world to come.

'Your Lordships most humble
and obedient Servant,
'JOHN GERARD.'

2. Assembly of the herbs

Gerard's great, awe-inspiring book on herbs and plants has had such a profound influence upon my thinking that I should like to describe it here so that you will know something about the way its information is presented. The *Herball* is of such magnificent scope and nature that nothing for the reader has yet appeared to equal it. To make this tremendous volume complete and readable, Gerard used wonderful illustrations showing the complete plant (the root, the stem, the flowers, and the seeds). Each plant was thus given a true identity about which there could be no question. To each plant he gave a botanical name and a common name. He told about the best time for planting and the type of soil best suited to each plant. He gave the origin of each plant and told how each one expanded through use all over the world. His next sections on each plant were 'Temperature', 'Virtues', and 'Use'.

The unsurpassed eloquence of his book starts this way:

'Courteous Reader,

'Here are many things which I think needful to impart unto thee, both concerning the knowledge of PLANTS in generall, also for better explaining of some things pertinent to the Histories, which I have set forth much amended and inlarged. For the great difference, affections, and etc. of Plants, I hold it not fitting nor necessary for me to insist upon them; neither do I intend in any large discourse to set forth their many and great uses and virtues: Give me leave only to tell you, That: God of his infinite goodness and bounty hath by the medium of Plants, best bestowed almost all food, clothing, and medicine on MAN.'

Gerard must have been an inspiration to everyone with whom he came in contact, either in person or through his *Herball*.

Brothers of the Spade, which contains the correspondence of Peter Collinson of London and John Custis of Williamsburg, Virginia, should also be explained at this point, at least in brief, because it shows us that plant exchange on a large scale was possible on an international basis even before the days of modern transportation. The correspond-ence, covering the period from 1734 to 1746 was collected and edited by E. G. Swem in 1948. Very simply, it is the story of how Mr Collin-son sent herbs and other plants from England to Mr Custis in America and how Mr Custis reciprocated by sending to Mr Collinson varieties of herbs and plants indigenous to America. Here is one of the letters, quoted verbatim as it appears on page 103:

London January 31: 1743/4

My Dear Sir
Colonel Custis
    I have only time to tell you that I have sent you a Box of sundry seed, for your Kitchen Garden & Beg the Box may be re-turn'd Filled with Cones of your Common Flowering poplar or Tulip Tree—and some Cassena Seed and any other sort you please, Pellitory in particular umbrella, papa, sweet flowering Bay. I shall in a particular manner thank You for the Box of seeds & all Came safe by Captain Friend and in good Order.

My Dear friend My best Wishes
Attends you from your affectionate
friend
P. Collinson
The box Comes by Captain Robinson
in the York

This one letter expresses the purpose of this section of my book: 'kitchen garden' is the key phrase because a part of every kitchen garden should be an herb garden. By growing herbs in the garden we can enjoy the beautiful blossoming flowers with their innate fragrance, and we can be assured of garden freshness in the kitchen when we want to use these palate-caressing flavours.

    In Genesis we are told: 'And God said, Let the earth bring forth grass, the herb yielding seed, *and* the fruit tree yielding fruit after his kind, whose seed *is* in itself, upon the earth: and it was so', and that in the earth there was 'every herb of the field'.

    Meditating on the perfect union of fragrance and flavour in these herbs of the field brings to mind a beautiful little poem:

Assembly of the herbs

For flowers that bloom about our feet,
For tender grass, so fresh, so sweet;
For song of bird and hum of bee,
For all things fair we hear or see,
Father in heaven, we thank Thee.

For blue of stream and blue of sky,
For pleasant shade of branches high,
For fragrant air and cooling breeze,
For beauty in the blooming trees,
Father in heaven, we thank Thee.

RALPH WALDO EMERSON

Rosemary is the traditional symbol of remembrance. Thousands of years ago, when the Mediterranean was the centre of the world, rosemary, one of the small blessings of the herb family, grew along the northern shores and on the many islands. I like to think of it adding its fragrance to the winds blowing out over the bright blue sea. I can almost see the simple herb gatherers going from place to place along the shores and around the islands in their primitive boats propelled by paddles, their rush baskets filling with sweet-smelling herbs such as anise, rosemary, savory, and many others to sell or trade with the adventurous Phoenician traders. Also in the picture are the Greeks and Sicilians who sailed the waters of the rippling Mediterranean in luxurious barges laden with products from their homeland to barter for treasures of this exotic region. With all of these priceless things afloat it was quite natural for piracy to thrive around Marseille, the principal port of the time. Those ships fortunate enough to avoid pirates sent their precious cargoes inland from Marseille.

I have been told that monks at the mountain monastery of La Grande Chartreuse in France planted the sweet-smelling herbs in borders around the flower beds as well as in the herb garden. As they walked softly among the tender blessings of the gardens, they decided to plant small low-growing herbs between the stepping-stones. When lightly trodden on, they would give of themselves completely, yielding from their innermost depths a lovely scent to make the evening stroll a fragrant and agreeable pleasure after the dew fell. Everyone is well aware of the fact that monks make the most delectable cordials in the world, flavoured with anise, mint, and many other herbs.

The art of cooking is almost as old as man himself, and even the earliest man soon learned that the pungent and aromatic little herb plants added a tantalizing bouquet to things eaten. As civilization progressed, these same age-old bouquets were achieved with sauces, stews, and desserts. In the recipe sections I include some of my special recipes that call for herbs.

A recent survey made by one of the world's largest spice houses says, 'Few women know how to use spices and herbs, therefore fear them. Yet it can be the difference between good and bad cooking. The standard spices of most women are pepper, nutmeg, mustard, cinnamon, cloves, garlic and celery salt, yet there are more than one hundred in use today.'

A FEW FACTS ABOUT HERB COOKING

A half teaspoon of dried herbs is equivalent to two scant teaspoons fresh. To bring out the aromatic oils lurking in the leaves, buds, and seeds, crush or chop fresh herbs before using; soak dried herbs in oil, wine, or broth, then crush.

Fine chopped herbs are called *fines herbes*.

A faggot of herbs is a bunch tied together, usually thyme, bay, and parsley.

A bouquet garni, frequently mentioned in French cooking, is a mixture of herbs and seasonings, usually parsley, thyme, bay leaves, celery, and leeks, tied in a cheesecloth bag and added to the cooking pot.

We may live without friends, we may live without books,
But civilized man cannot live without cooks.

ARISTIPPUS

3. Herbs tell their stories

AMBROSIA
Oke of Cappadocia

This fragrant herb from Asia Minor moved the poets in ancient times to suppose that it was meat and food for the gods and that it conferred immortality on mortals who ate it. This is an indication of the tremendously interesting and varied background of ambrosia.

Pliny, the Roman, said that ambrosia is a wandering name, often given to other herbs—a prime example being botrys, otherwise known as the oke of Paradise or the oke of Jerusalem; it has also been given to the Mexican tea (*Chenopodium ambrosioides*), which is made into a nectar delicious in both taste and aroma.

Ambrosia has many virtues. It has been used as a medicine for coughs and colds. The leaves can be candied or made into a conserve. The leaves give a divine flavour to the famous ambrosia dessert made with fresh grated coconut and fresh orange sections for the traditional Christmas feast. The leaves, dried and laid among garments, not only smell sweet but protect them from moths and silverfish. No herb garden is complete without the romantic and heavenly fragrance of the oke of Cappadocia . . . and its misty lace-like foliage will enhance the beauty of all the other plants in the garden. Once you have it growing it needs very little attention as too much cultivation will kill it.

Here is the beautiful description of ambrosia by Dioscorides, the Greek physician: 'It groweth to the height of two cubits, yealding many weak, crooked and streaked branches, dividing themselves into sundry other small branches, having from the middle to the top thereof many mossie yellowish floures, standing one before the other in good order. And the whole plant is as if it were covered with a bran or mealy dust: the floures doe change into small cornered buttons, much like unto Tribulus Terrestris; wherein is contained black and round seeds, pleasant in taste and smell: the leaves are shaped like the leaves of mugwort, but thinner and more tender: all the whole plant is hoary, and yealdeth a pleasant savor: the whole plant perished with me at the first approach of winter.'

I shall add—more than all of this has been proved of ambrosia!

ANGELICA
Archangelica
officinalis
of the carrot family

Angelica was one of the first 'wonder' drugs, but today it has been largely replaced in herbal medicine by more specific plants. Of all the herbs I have looked into, particularly from the standpoint of medicinal use, none were in the early herbals described as having even one half of the medicinal uses attributed to the roots of angelica. Here are just a few of these uses: angelica root is a singular remedy against poison and the plague; just holding a piece of the root in the mouth will chase

23

away anything that could be bothering one; the root also opens the liver and spleen; a decoction of the root made in wine is good for the cold agues; it is good for the heart and will also cleanse the system thoroughly; the root is reported to cure the bites of mad dogs and all other venomous beasts—the list goes on and on.

There are several varieties of angelica, and to simplify matters we shall describe the one called garden angelica from here on. It seems to grow best in the northern temperate regions and New Zealand. The angelica plant is most unusual in its architecture. From the roots, very great thick and hollow stalks spring up, sometimes as high as six or seven feet. They are jointed or kneed in appearance and other arms and branches develop from these joints. Tufts of whitish flowers grow at the top of the branches shooting out from the joints; the flowers bloom during the months of July and August. The garden angelica is used primarily in California sweet white wines and tonics—and the roots are generally powdered and used in rose jars and sachets. The primary use of the stalks is in making angelica candy.

Another variety of angelica, called wild angelica, is grown in Great Britain. The British use the roots for medicinal purposes and in the preparation of gin.

Although there is very little use for angelica in the home, many things we bring into our homes contain it, so we should learn to appreciate it more and more. Knowledge often makes for warmth of heart. See page 123 for Angelica recipe.

ANISE
Pimpinella anisum
of the carrot family

This is one herb that almost everyone has come in contact with at one time or another, probably without knowing it, since the taste of licorice and the word 'anise' have been associated very infrequently by most people. It is a must for the kitchen herb garden because of its many uses. The oil from the seeds of anise is in great demand by drug houses because it is an excellent flavouring for all kinds of medical preparations and children seem to like it particularly.

Foxhounds are familiar with anise to a certain degree . . . especially those that are used in a drag hunt. The trend in drag hunting is to lay an artificial scent by saturating a sack in anise oil and having a horse and rider make a lay trail by dragging the artificial scent a mile or two across the countryside. Two leader hounds are taught the fox scent as well as the artificial scent. The leaders are used to train the pack for the drag and the real hunt. Drag hunts help to maintain enthusiasm on the part of the hounds, the horses, and the hunting men for the sport of the challenge cup race, the steeplechase, and riding to the hounds in pursuit of a fox.

Anise is native to southwestern Asia, northern Africa, and southeastern Europe but it has been introduced into the temperate regions of both hemispheres. It is an unusual plant in that it never seems to stray from its garden; so far as can be ascertained, it has never been found growing wild. It is mentioned frequently in the Scriptures and we know it has been cultivated for more than two thousand years. In the ninth century Charlemagne commanded that it be planted and grown upon the imperial farms. Many Greek and Roman authors, such as Dioscorides, Theophrastus, Pliny, and Palladius, wrote extensively about its use and cultivation.

Anise is a magnificent specimen of nature and will beautify any garden. It generally grows to a height of about eighteen inches and bears small yellowish-white flowers. The stems are slender and cylindrical, very erect and branchy, and the stem leaves are more and more finely cut toward the upper part. The fruits or 'seeds' of anise are greenish grey in colour and their shape is ovoid or oblong. For growing purposes, the seeds should never be more than two years old and should be planted as soon as the weather becomes settled in early spring.

The various parts of the anise plant have many uses. The leaves are frequently used for garnishing and flavouring salads. To a smaller extent, they are used as potherbs. The seeds are used on a far larger scale. Their flavouring power is so strong that they must be used sparingly to avoid overpowering other flavours present. The seeds are used as a flavour in various condiments, especially curry powders, many kinds of cake, pastry, and confectionery, and in some kinds of cheeses and breads. The oil extracted from the seeds is in great demand and is generally obtained by distillation with water. About one pound of oil is obtained from fifty pounds of seeds. This oil is also widely used in making perfumes, and various combinations of anise with other materials are used for sachets, perfumed soaps, and many toilet articles.

Look at one of the 'Suggested Patterns for Growing' in Chapter 5 to see where anise will fit into your plans. Remember that with anise, as with most of the herbs, you will have wonderful balmy beauty outside as well as an aromatic flavour in the kitchen.

BALM
(Lemon Balm)
Melissa
officinalis
of the mint family

What could be more delightful than to have little Melissa flavouring our finger bowls or giving to our iced tea her green beauty, her very lemonlike flavour, and her fragrance that is pure freshness? This lovely aroma has been used in medicines, liqueurs, potpourri, cooking, and beverages. The bees, who are known for being particular, greatly appreciate the abundant nectar of the flowers as much as we like the sweet aromatic leaf. The flowers are a beautiful purplish white and they appear on the plant in well-formed clusters.

This beloved perennial is a native of southern Europe but it is now found growing in nearly all temperate climates throughout the world. The plant grows to a height of about two feet and the bright green crinkled leaves possess a scent that makes the ardent gardener and the flower arranger alike want to give it a choice spot in the herb garden. It is truly another one of the 'little blessings' of the kitchen garden, and for the apartment house dweller it is ideal to grow in a pot or will do very nicely in a window box.

An old Arabian proverb conveyed this promise: 'It makes the heart merry and joyful.' For a delightful, sweet-and-spicy drink to dispel melancholy, the leaves may be heavily steeped in water. For a more delicate drink with the same flavour (but less of it), the leaves should be allowed to remain in the water for a very short time. This one should be served with thin lemon slices and sugar. Lemon balm will also make either hot or iced tea develop a more pleasing bouquet. One of the first things you should do with the lemon balm plant is to try some of the tender sprigs or leaves in fruit cups or salads.

BERGAMOT
(Bee Balm)
Monarda didyma
of the mint family

A long, long time ago a ruby-throated hummingbird was flying from his home in the North to visit in the South. When he had completed about half of the journey he decided it was time to look for something to eat. He saw a field of flowers in the distance and soared toward them as fast as his wings could carry him. As he drew nearer and nearer he was almost overwhelmed by the brilliant colour of the flowers. They had seemed pale pink from above, but now they were literally bursting their petals with vibrant red. The humming-bird felt certain that anything so beautiful would have a refreshing nectar to match. His first sip was so delectable and satisfying that he sipped and sipped to the bursting point. He was so pleasantly satisfied that he hurried to tell the butterflies and the bees. He described the flower heads as resembling the honeycomb. Later the mischievous bees told the wasps how to pierce holes in the bottom of the tubes of the honeycomb flower heads to steal the nectar from the hummingbirds and the butterflies.

Bergamot is a showy plant that grows in dry soil or thickets. It is colourful in flower arrangements or herb borders. It is a perennial and generally grows to a height of two to three feet. The plant exudes a rich mint essence.

A delicious tea can be made from the pungent tender leaves of bergamot; it was used on a large scale for tea when early colonists boycotted English imports. The colonists had learned of this tea from the Oswego Indians and named it Oswego tea after this tribe.

Bergamot has many uses: as garnish for wine cups and fruit punch bowls; as a flavourful ingredient in salads (delicious when used lightly); as a potpourri; and the French are said to use it sometimes as a flavouring.

WOOD
BETONY
Betonica officinalis
or *Stachys betonica*
of the mint family

Many years ago while perusing one of the old and famous herbals, I saw the name 'betony' and was struck at once by its poetical sound and spelling. The name was so intriguing that I felt an urge to know personally the plant that carried this beautiful name. It has had a prominent spot in the wild-flower section of my herb garden ever since and, happily, the plant and the name formed the perfect synonym. The stem of this particular Betonica grows to a height of approximately twelve inches; it leaves are long and broad with a deep dark green hue. Snow-white flowers appear in June and remain throughout July. There is another type of Betonica that is similar to the one just described except that it has purple and red flowers.

Betony is a native of Europe and found most of its usefulness in the field of medicine. The monks of old distilled simples from herbs, and the 'vertues' of betony rated very high. A few of them are:

Makes for a good stomach and appetite for meat. Brings on good humor. Good against the pain of sciatica or ache of knuckle bone. Cures bitings of mad dogs, good for ruptures, cramps and convulsions. Most singular against poison, supposed to break stones in kidneys. Good against falling sickness and singular against all pains of the head.

COMMON
SPEEDWELL
Veronica officinalis

The Common Speedwell is known in the United States as Paul's betony. Its stems range from three inches to ten inches in length. The flowers which stay on the plant from May to August, are very small, beautiful pale blue, and crowded on long spikes. It prefers dry fields, uplands, and open woods.

An ancient legend of the medieval flower lovers is that a maiden saw Jesus on his way to Calvary and, observing the suffering on his face, thought she would wipe away some of the anguish with her handkerchief, which was scented with speedwell or betony. It has been declared that ever afterward the handkerchief bore the imprint of Jesus' sacred features. Of course special healing virtues were attributed to the handkerchief, and it became one of the most precious relics at

St Peter's in Rome. Since very few people could go to Rome to be cured by the handkerchief, the roadside plant was named for St Paul the apostle.

BORAGE
Borago officinalis
of the Boraginaceae
family

Borage is a 'cool' herb, imparting that touch to salads, lemonade, and other cooling drinks. The fresh foliage has a flavour very much like that of the cucumber. It is native to the Mediterranean, like so many of its brothers and sisters. It has been naturalized throughout the civilized world by Europeans who cultivated it originally more for medicinal than culinary purposes. Like angelica and lovage, borage was at one time considered what we would call a 'wonder drug' today but, like the others, it has managed to throw off the superstitions and unfounded medicinal uses attributed to it.

It was listed by Peter Martyr, according to the Scottish poet Hew Ainslie, as having been planted on Isabella Island by Columbus' companions. It is very probable that borage was brought to America by the colonists during Queen Elizabeth's time. It first appeared in American seedsmen's catalogues in 1806.

The case of borage, and others like it, is one of the primary reasons this book was written. Borage is a wonderfully versatile plant that gives fragrance and beauty in the garden *and* fragrance and flavour in the kitchen. Yet the demand for it has always been small, and it is quite possible that most people have not become aware of its culinary uses, having always thought of it in terms of medicine if they thought of it at all.

No other plant is more easily grown than borage and it flowers so freely that it is ideal for a bee forage. This is just one of the bonus uses offered by borage. It is a somewhat branchy, hairy plant that generally grows to a height of one and a half feet. The oval leaves and other green parts are covered with whitish, rather sharp hairs. The flowers are in clusters and are sky blue, a truly beautiful shade that will enhance any garden and particularly any herb garden. The seed will grow in any soil, but borage seems to have a preference for light, dry soils, waste places, and steep banks, where it develops more flavour.

The tender upper leaves and flowers are used to a large extent in salads, to which they impart an always enjoyable but seldom recognizable flavour. It is because of borage's ability to blend so subtly that few people are aware of what they are enjoying. The lower, mature leaves are cooked like spinach and it is just as full of vitamins and energy, with a cool, cucumber taste.

BURNET
*Sanguisorba
minor*
of the rose family

Little burnet came originally from Europe and Asia, bringing with it a fragrance of fresh greens and a flavour resembling fresh cucumbers. It is not very well known in the United States. It is a perennial with large low-spreading leaves that present a dark green underneath and a lighter green above. These will generally cover an area measuring about two feet across the top. The flowers come in June and are of a reddish copper colour, with stems that reach upward to a height of twelve to fifteen inches. The little flowers have been called weather prophets because before a storm, on a cloudy day, they fold their petals and hide.

The young leaves make a beautifully compatible mixture with tarragon and rosemary. This would make a good starting point for those meeting burnet for the first time. Burnet is included in recipes for spiced vinegars, cooked greens, green salads, cream and cottage cheese, and it makes a zestful cup of tea.

CALAMUS
Acorus calamus
marsh herb
of the arum family

This perennial plant with its fragrant leaves and roots came to us from Syria and Egypt and the history, adventure, and romance connected with it are quite without parallel. It has been called the true aromatic reed of the ancients, who used these reeds as writing pens. It has been referred to as being a viceroy but could well be called a king among plants. It grows best in marshland or very wet places but will do very well in ordinary garden soil.

Calamus, often known as sweet flag, has been in high esteem since the very earliest days of our civilization. It was written about in the Song of Solomon. John Gerard, whose fame dates back to the sixteenth and seventeenth century, wrote at great length about calamus. Here is one quaint remark he made about it:

It is boiled also in baths for women, and decoctions for Clisters, and it enters into plaisters and perfumes for the smells sake.

Ladies of colonial times grew calamus in their herb gardens especially for its leaves, which were used in creams, puddings, and custards. The roots were used during that period to keep moths and insects out of closets where clothing and furs were stored. Today the roots are widely used in perfumes and medicines, which necessitates our importing many, many tons per year. In the field of medicine, the calamus root is still in wide demand the world over, especially in Britain and the United States, for use in a home remedy for colic.

Enjoyment of its fragrance is more than sufficient reason for growing this plant, and it is easily propagated from division of the roots. In the case of older plants, the roots are often several feet long and two inches thick—and this makes calamus ideal for plant exchange with neighbours and other friends.

CAMOMILE
Anthemis nobilis
of the aster family

This is one of three different plants bearing the name 'camomile', and the one most widely grown because it is more adaptable to changing soil and climate. *Anthemis nobilis* (and perhaps the other two camomiles as well) has been cultivated for more than two thousand years as a combination ground cover and beautifying ornament.

Camomile is quite different from most of the other herbs, both in appearance and in internal make-up. Its stems like to stay close to mother earth, and they weave their way along, rooting as they go. The stems of the flowers reach upward about one foot above the ground and are topped with daisylike blossoms, with white florets surrounding a yellow centre disc. The leaves are many and fernlike, much divided, so that they tend to form mats at each rooting spot of the creeping plant stem. They are grey-green and make an ideal ground cover for pathways. In fact it is said that many of our very old gardens had raised mounds of earth covered with the mossy-looking camomile, which made a soft and comfortable place to sit.

Camomile can be used in most areas that will not support the growth of grass. It is a very hardy perennial, native to the northern shores of the Mediterranean, and both the foliage and the flower heads are very aromatic. The dried flower heads are the only parts of the plant utilized commercially. An oil is extracted from them that is an

C

important ingredient of many hair preparations and shampoos. The dried flower heads are also used in making camomile tea, which is a valuable carminative—a soother of stomach disturbances and yet a wonderfully tasty beverage, said to be good for the complexion.

Camomile flowers practically all summer. It is suggested that it be used in your herb garden (or flower garden, for that matter) as an edging or ground cover. And remember that camomile fills the surrounding air with a pleasing, pungent fragrance.

Another of the three camomiles is one called the German camomile (*Matricaria chamomilla*) which has antiseptic and healing properties. An oil is extracted from the dried flower heads which is used in medicine as an emetic. The third one differs from the plain camomile (*Anthemis nobilis*), sometimes referred to as the Roman camomile, only in that it has a double row of white ray florets in its blossoms.

Anthemis nobilis has been called the 'apple of the earth'. My English grandmother made camomile tea by steeping the fresh or dried leaves as you would any tea leaf (three teaspoons fresh or one dried in her cup). She would serve the children at the party one half cup camomile tea and one half cup hot milk with sugar. We knew this as cambric tea.

CARAWAY
Carum carvi
of the carrot family

Caraway is almost unique, at least from the standpoint of history, in that it is one of the very, very few herbs that created a friendly rivalry between cooks and doctors, each vying to give it more prominence than the other. Now the cooks seem to be in the lead, since there are many culinary uses for caraway while only one primary usage remains in the field of medicine: to disguise the flavour of repulsive drugs.

At one time it was believed that caraway was a native of Asia Minor, but it seems well established now that actually it first came from

Europe. Twelfth-century writings describe its growth in Morocco and they also point out that the Arabs grew it in the thirteenth century. Apparently the use of caraway spread first with the Phoenician commerce to western Europe and from there throughout the rest of the civilized world. It has been so very widely distributed that it is possible to find it almost any place on the globe.

Caraway is one of the 'herby' herbs, with everything to offer from the standpoint of fragrance, flavour, and beauty. It is biennial or annual but it self-sows itself year after year by dropping or exploding seeds. It can be very easily grown from seed and it germinates readily. The following description of the plant itself will tend to make you aware of its beauty in the garden, its utility in the kitchen, and its usefulness in making flower arrangements. The plant has a fleshy root that is yellowish on the outside and whitish on the inside, with a slight taste of carrots. From this root a rosette of finely divided leaves is developed and at a later date the sparsely leafed, hollow, branching flower stems bear umbels of small white flowers. The stems will reach a height of between eighteen and thirty inches and this is the main reason for using the caraway plant in flower arrangements. After the flowers come the oblong, light brown, aromatic fruits that are the caraway 'seeds' of commerce.

The caraway seed is one of the most widely used seeds in the world and can be found in rye bread, cake, cheese, German sauerkraut, apple pie, baked apples, and cabbage soups. Caraway can be sugar-coated for confectionery to be munched after meals as a preventive of indigestion. It also goes into perfumes, various toilet preparations, liqueurs, soaps, and, as mentioned earlier, is used to disguise the flavour of medicine that is difficult to take. The young roots of the caraway plant are sometimes boiled as vegetables. A pale yellow essential oil is distilled with water from the seeds, which normally contain between five per cent and seven and one half per cent of the oil.

It is used medicinally as an aid to digestion and included in medicine prescribed for a variety of gastric troubles. Many agricultural seedsmen include it in mixtures for temporary pastures or herbal leys of the kind increasingly used by modern organic farmers.

Complete and simple growing instructions may be found in Chapter 5.

CATNIP
Nepeta cataria
of the mint family

This is one herb that has shown remarkable popularity down through the ages although it does not possess the blending, flavour-imparting fragrance of thyme or sage or any of the most widely used herbs of today. It is mentioned here because it is definitely a part of the herb picture and is also a well-known 'weed'. The Greeks and Romans grew it to make their cats happy, but there is much more reason for growing it today. It is a stately, ornamental plant that will add beautiful white clusters of flowers to an herb garden from June to August. In earlier days catnip was used in making tea for infants and beverages for adults. It was also used as a tranquillizer for babies.

It was native to Europe and western Asia but has been naturalized over most of the civilized countries. It will grow with practically no care in any fairly dry soil. Seed can be sown either in the fall or spring and all that is needed is to keep the weeds down. The stems grow to a height of eighteen to thirty-six inches.

Actually, a fairly large number of cooks still use catnip as a seasoning. The foliage has a faint aromatic scent not unlike that of lemons. It is an herb that requires special 'know-how' of use and this know-how comes only with experience. First, plant it in your herb garden (or any garden) for its ornamental value and the great pleasure it brings to cats. Then, when time permits, start working it into some of your established seasoning mixtures and sauces. A pleasant surprise will be yours.

CHERVIL
Anthriscus
cerefolium
of the carrot family

This is a distinguished name, and one that will always draw the respect of the discriminating people who use chervil so wisely and delectably. It is a native of southern Europe and is a milder form of parsley, which some think has been overused. The gastronomically wise French have always been the largest users of chervil. They think so much of it that it is now in their world-famous combination of *fines herbes*. Some of the other European countries are becoming more chervil-conscious and the English are only slightly behind the French in appreciation of its wonderful attributes. It is not widely grown in the United States as yet, but it is the type of herb that could 'catch on' quickly, once more is generally known about it.

The chervil plant is easily grown from seed and, unlike other members of the parsley family, the seed germinates readily. It will grow to a height of twelve to twenty-four inches in most sections of the country. The stems shoot out many, many branches that bear very finely cut, much-divided, almost lacelike leaves. The flowers are white and tiny, with the white florets arranged in small umbels. The seeds that follow are long and black. The plant resembles parsley in growth and appearance and looks well in any herb garden.

Only the leaves are used today but in ages past Pliny thought that hiccoughs could be stopped by drinking vinegar containing the seed of chervil. Parkinson, some of whose writings appear in *Brothers of the Spade*, said that 'some recommend the green seeds sliced and put in a sallet of herbs and eaten with vinegar and oil, to comfort a cold stomach of the aged.'

The whole chervil plant has a delightful aniselike fragrance; its flavour resembles that of anise with a very light sprinkling of pepper. Chervil leaves in salad are widely used in France. The effect of the leaves in potato salad is matchless. They are also used as a condiment

37

in soups, egg dishes, and on fish. They are found in many sauces, particularly in béarnaise and ravigote, and they greatly enhance butter sauces for chicken and wine and butter sauce for cutlets.

You will be pleased with chervil in your herb garden and in your kitchen.

CHICORY
Cichorium intybus
of the Compositae
family

> *On a dewy morning or through a cloudy day*
> *These blue and starlike flowers brighten up our way.*

These clear, bright blue flowers are found in unexpected places such as fields, waste places, and along roadsides. Chicory has grown wild in these places since it was naturalized in the United States. It is a native of Europe, but it is said that the name 'chicory' comes from the Arabic *chicourey*.

Chicory has an unusual background in that it seems to have gone through cycles down through the centuries of use and cultivation. In fact, during the late 1800s and 1900s, chicory was launched as a huge farm crop in America. This development came about through a prejudice on the part of the principal users, who at that time happened to be European immigrants. They felt that the American-grown chicory was inferior to that obtainable from Europe on a duty-free basis. In 1898 or '99 advantage was taken of a protective duty and several factories were constructed in the United States. Farmers were alerted in advance and had large crops (roots) available when the first factories were finished. The entire project was abandoned after a few years because there was not enough profit in the operation, despite government help.

Today, chicory is grown as a farm crop for the roots, which are dried and ground for use with coffee. In the beginning, ground chicory was used to 'adulterate' coffee and quite possibly there may still exist coffee 'adulteration' on a fairly large scale. Certain sections of the country, however, such as New Orleans and its environs, prefer a mixture of chicory and coffee to the pure product, and sizeable companies have been marketing a chicory-coffee blend on the retail level for several years.

There is scarcely a part of the chicory plant that has not been used at one time or another. The young roots have been cooked as carrots and served with butter, salt, and pepper. The stalks have been blanched by heaping soil around the base of the plant and eaten like celery. The young leaves of the chicory plant have been eaten in salads and as greens. A special strain of chicory called Brussels witloof is available today as a plant or seed. It is a perennial and the roots can be dried and used as a substitute for coffee; the leaves are used when young and tender as greens or those of the older plants are blanched in much the same way as celery. The best-known foliage of chicory used for salads or greens is called witloof. To get the crown of uncoloured leaves now known as witloof, the roots are trimmed on the lower end to a length of eight or nine inches, then placed upright in soil or sand in a box. The crown is covered with about eight inches of sand and the temperature is kept at 60° F. In two or three weeks the white salad witloof should be ready, a good 'head' being six inches long.

Chicory is a very handsome plant, rangy by nature, and has clean green leaves that seem to be content in their supporting role. The star, of course, deserves the role she is playing. She is that beautiful, bright, clear blue dainty flower that started this story, although types with white, pink, or purple flowers appear now and then. The flowers are in bloom from July to September or October and they open their petals for the world to see the intricate workmanship inside only when the sun is shining, and then only until noon, or on a dark day.

Perhaps the greatest use of chicory today is by farmers who value the medicinal and nutritional effects of deep-rooting herbs in grazing pastures for cattle, sheep, and pigs. It is loved by these animals and its deep roots draw up from the subsoil minerals and trace elements not available to the animal from shallower rooting grasses and clovers. (See *Fertility Pastures* (Faber and Faber), by Newman Turner.)

CHIVES
Allium
schoenoprasum
of the lily family

'Chives bring forth many leaves about a hand-full high, long, slender, round like to little rushes; amongst which grow up small and tender stalkes, sending forth certaine Knops with floures like those of the onion, but much lesser. They have many little bulbes or headed roots fastened together: out of which grow down into the earth a great number of little strings, and it hath both the smell and taste of the onion and leeke, as if it were participating of both.' That is Gerard's quaint and accurate description of chives.

In all probability, salads were eaten before chives knocked on the door of the 'Green Rooms' asking to be let in. The fact that they were let in and became reigning king of the salad bowl is well known to all.

Chives were first grown in European gardens during the sixteenth century and entered our gardens sometime before the year 1806. It is seen in well-kept records that chives began colonizing the American salad during the latter part of the eighteenth century and, of course, they have maintained rigid control of it during the country's growth. In the early gardens of Virginia this small ornamental perennial plant was used for borders. The delicate violet-pink clover-like blooms were used in bouquets and the tender blades were cut for making butter sauces and salads. In the fall, clumps would be lifted and potted for the window garden since the dried leaves of chives are useless.

Chives are very closely related to the onion, having just about the same aroma and taste, though far milder, and in physical appearance the only real difference is in the size of the bulbous base. Practically everyone is familiar with the various sizes of onions available and, in comparison to even the smallest onion, the base of a chive is much smaller and looks like the slightly swollen base of the stem. In my garden chives grow to a height of about six inches and the leaves, or hollow tubes, have a yellow-green colour.

Chives have a magic name among chefs, and it is difficult to find one who would be without them, because they seem to work miracles in any dish that needs a light touch of onion flavour. They are particularly delectable in salads and omelets and give the taste buds a change without making them do somersaults. There are so many culinary uses for chives that only a few of these are mentioned but they are representative: cheeses, soups, potato salad, fish, spaghetti, and various vegetables. I hope this will spur you to experiment in your kitchen, after having grown them, keeping the tops cut for fresh new growth.

They should be permanant fixtures in your herb garden. A fresh, continuous supply can be purchased in the stores in the spring or autumn.

CLARY
Salvia sclarea
of the mint family

A native of the Mediterranean, clary is definitely a part of any herb picture, though it has now settled into a less prominent spot than it occupied during the old days of herb use. The herb gardener of today will be interested primarily in clary as an ornamental source of pleasantly different fragrance, a spicy fragrance that is similar to that found in sage, to which it is closely related.

It is a biennial and will not flower until the second season, but the leaves can be harvested at any time. The leaves are not so much used today in culinary practice because much of the flavour is lost in cooking. They are still used sometimes in omelets and the flowers find their way into aromatic teas. Rhenish wines in Germany at one time owed their muscatel raisin flavour to a combination of clary leaves and elder flowers. *Muscateller sallier* is the German name for clary and means muscatel sage.

Commercially, clary is a most important herb. Very widely used in perfumery and in making sachets is clary sage oil, which is extracted from the leaves, of which the smaller and uppermost are richest in the essential oil.

During the seventeenth and eighteenth centuries the fragrance and flavour were so highly prized that many noted tavern keepers in London gave their patrons all manner of food and drink containing clary. There is no record of the reaction of the patrons to this clary treatment but, since it continued for so long and with the same patrons, it must have been one of complete satisfaction. As with most of the older herbs, many unusual traits were at various times attributed to clary. Among these was the thought that clary was good for 'weak backs and to straighten the reins being made into tansies and eaten otherwise.' It has been listed in seedsmen's catalogues since 1806.

It is an important ingredient of some botanic eye lotions and an infusion of the dried leaves is beneficial for bathing tired eyes.

Picture the ornamental effect, perhaps as a flower border, from the following description of the plant. The stems are square and covered with hairs that look like shiny wires; they reach a height of two to three feet. The leaves present a singular spectacle, being large and very broad on the lower part of the stems and becoming smaller as they ascend the stem. They are greyish green, oblong in shape, obtuse, opposite, and woolly-haired. The flowers arrive in June of the second season and remain in bloom almost all summer. They are lilac or greenish white, very showy, and have a perfume that is almost over-powering. They are borne in numerous conspicuous spikes twelve inches or more in length over the upper half of the plant. Here are beauty and fragrance of an unusual nature, just waiting to grace your garden.

CORIANDER
*Coriandrum
sativum*
of the carrot family

This herb, which has been of such great importance to mankind, has been cultivated so long that it is now doubtful that its origin can be ascertained with even a measure of accuracy. The seeds of coriander are probably the most unusual of all the herbs. When the seeds have ripened and are dried, they develop a scent and flavour resembling orange, anise, and cumin. Their bouquet is so very desirable and savoury that it has been described in the following ways by different professional people in the cooking field: 'sweet and tart . . . extremely pleasant . . . lemon peel with sage odour', and as we mentioned just above, 'resembles strongly the effect of mixing orange, anise, and cumin'. The seeds are so good that we import over three million pounds annually.

Coriander seeds have been found in Egyptian tombs of the Twenty-first Dynasty. They were well known in Pliny's time and he wrote that the best seeds came to Italy from Egypt. At one time in the dim past it was thought that the use of coriander caused people to become avaricious, but this was undoubtedly tied in with the super-stitions that so often were associated with herbs used medicinally. Eventually it was decided that coriander has practically no medical value, but at one time it was sprinkled over meat to keep it from spoil-ing. Just for the record, coriander was planted in America by the earliest colonists and was actually planted within our shores before the year 1670.

The plant resembles anise in some respects. Slightly divided leaves at the base form the foundation for branching stems that grow to a height of about two and one half feet. Near the top the leaves are much divided and in these are found linear segments of small rosy-white or plain white flowers. Next comes a pair of brownish-yellow seeds that are about the size of a pea seed. Always remember that the seeds are to be ripened and dried before use. Coriander likes warm, friable soil best although it will do a good job of plant production in most any good soil. Seed has been planted in the fall with success but it is recognized that springtime is better for planting. The seeds appear about ninety days after sowing and should not be picked until it is distinctly brown. It is at this time that the fruiting clusters should be cut and dried. Many seeds will be lost if left too long on the plant. They should be stored in very tightly stoppered containers.

One of the primary uses for the seed is as one of the innumerable ingredients of curry powder. It is used in flavouring pickles, in the manufacture of liquors, and in meats, sausages, sauces, bread, cookies, and confectionery. It also makes pea soup delectable. Biscuits and poultry stuffing are greatly enhanced by the seed. Apple pie is more delicious with it; and try rubbing it on pork before roasting. It makes tossed chef's salad truly delightful and it does the same for some Mexican dishes also.

COSTMARY
Chrysanthemum balsamita
of the Compositae family

We can give our thanks to western Asia for producing this tall, beautiful, stately-looking plant. When you consider the over-all architectural structure of costmary, there is no handsomer plant for the herb garden. It grows to a height of three feet or more but is rather woody and sprawling unless cut back frequently. Most people who are fortunate enough to have costmary in their herb gardens cut the young leaves very often and this has a twofold effect: number one, it keeps the plant within the range of garden beauty; and number two, the younger leaves are far more succulent than the older ones.

From the standpoint of pure fragrance there is no herb that can equal costmary in the garden. Even without bruising the leaves between the fingers, there is always evident a lovely scent of a combination of lemon, chrysanthemum, and mint. It is thought of as one of the most fragrant of all herbs.

Costmary is a hardy perennial that dies to the ground every winter but at the first signs of spring it is up again; it seems to like a dry, sunny situation. The leaves are rather large at the lower part of the plant and become smaller as the top is approached. These leaves are a beautiful green with a tinge of grey and a slight downy appearance. Incidentally, the dried leaves make a good tea. Costmary blooms in August and the flowers are beautiful, with a yellow centre and a white outer floret or series of florets.

Costmary has been known to man almost since the beginning of recorded history and has been grown for many, many centuries in Europe. It is a very highly aromatic plant throughout and in cookery it should be used sparingly; for example, one recipe that has come to light calls for but one costmary leaf for an entire meat or vegetable stew.

The history of the common and botanical names of this plant is interesting. *Balsamita* comes from the balsamic odour of the plant and 'costmary' comes from costus, a violet-scented plant from the Himalayas. The roots of this plant are used to prepare a very expensive perfume. The 'mary' part of the name comes from the Virgin Mary, to whom the plant seems to have been dedicated in most European countries. Various writings from the fifteenth century tell us that costmary was a very popular plant at that time and was exported from Spain to all parts of the world.

Costmary in the herb garden is a valuable and stately herb, its fragrance unequalled. In cookery, when used sparingly, it can make a great contribution to our eating habits. It is suggested that you grow costmary in your herb garden, first to look at and then, after a time has passed, take part of the leaf structure into the kitchen and experiment with it. You will find that there are many untold treasures lying there just for the asking.

CRESSES of the mustard family

Winter or Upland Cress (*Barbarea vulgaris*)
Water Cress (*Nasturtium officinalis*)
Garden Cress (*Lepidium sativum*)

We know that spring is really here when we see the crisp jade green of the upland cress shining forth, followed shortly thereafter by the water and garden types.

UPLAND or
WINTER CRESS
Barbarea vulgaris
of the cruciferae or
mustard family

This is the true upland or winter cress, as it is sometimes called. It should not be confused with water cress, which it resembles. Nor should it be confused with fine curled cress, which is also called pepper-grass. Upland cress has also been called dry-land or land cress. The names 'creasy salad' and 'highland creasy' have also crept into the naming picture in certain areas of Virginia where upland and a similar botanical variety grow as weeds. If the seeds of the upland are sown in early spring in rich soil, the leaves are ready for use in late summer. It is a hardy perennial and will have another crop of leaves for you in the spring. Gerard says this about it: 'It groweth in gardens among pot herbs, and very common in the fields neere unto paths and highwaies almost every where.' Make the most of the succulent freshness of the earliest of spring salad greens!

WATER CRESS
Nasturtium officinalis
of the Cruciferae or
mustard family

True water cress trailing in wet ground and springs makes a picture that is mouth-watering. It is the aristocrat of the cresses and is easily grown from seed. Water cress is best for greens when cut for use in early spring or autumn. Gerard mentioned this about it: 'Water cress is evidently hot and dry; and should be eaten in March when it's at its best, says M. Gooyer.' Sharpen your appetite with this delightful concept of a dainty titbit—the WATER CRESS SANDWICH—prepared as follows: Use very thin sliced bread (white or brown) and sweet butter. Cream the butter and spread it generously on the bread. Chill and wash cress carefully and spread on bread nicely. Fascinating!

Gerard also says: 'Water-cress hath many fat and weake hollow branches trailing upon the gravell & earth where it groweth, taking hold in sundry places as it creepeth; by means whereof the plant spreads over the great compasse of ground. The leaves are likewise compact and winged with many small leaves set upon a middle rib one against another, except the point leafe, which stands by its selfe, as doth the ash, if it grow in his natural place, which is in a gravelly Spring. The upper face of the whole plant is of a browne colour, and greene under leaves, which is a perfect marke to know the physicall kinde from the others. The white floures grow alongst the stalkes, and are succeeded by cods wherein the seed is contained. The root is nothing else but as it were a thrum or bundle of threds.'

GARDEN CRESS
Lepidum sativum

You are always assured of that new, fresh crispness in the leaf of the cress if you plant an annual, and garden cress is an annual. It grows quickly and makes wonderful greens for salads, cooking, or garnish for meats and salads. Then eat the garnish for zestful energy! And remember, the richer the soil, the better the plant.

All of the cresses are full of vitamins.

CUMIN
Cuminum cyminum
of the carrot family

It is difficult to find another herb of such ancient vintage or of so varied a historical background as cumin. It is mentioned in Matthew 23:23 that cumin, along with dill and mint, were used in tithing. Many of its earliest uses back in the days of Isaiah were more fancied than real, such as its powers to keep lovers from being fickle and to keep poultry from straying. As time passed, however, cumin came into its own . . . to such a point that Pliny is said to have considered it the best appetizer of all condiments. It was extremely popular during the Middle Ages and it is written about extensively and glowingly by all of the writers of the older herbals of the sixteenth and seventeenth centuries.

Cumin makes an ideal border plant, since it is diminutive and seldom exceeds a height of six inches. It is multi-stemmed, has linear-leaved foliage and small lilac flowers, in little umbels of ten to twenty blossoms each. The seeds resemble those of caraway and coriander, and have long hairs that fold up when the seed is dry.

The records show that cumin is native to the Nile Valley, but it has been cultivated in the Mediterranean region, Africa, Egypt,

Morocco, India, China, and Palestine from very early times. Today it is extensively cultivated in Malta and Sicily. It is also grown to some extent in the United States. The greatest single use of cumin today is as an ingredient of curry powder. The ground seeds go into many things, such as chili sauce and cheeses; they also find their way into the flavouring of pickles and soups.

The cumin plant has a strong aromatic fragrance and its taste is hot. When used correctly—and by this is meant proper blending and sparing use—cumin is a wonderfully versatile herb to have around. You will find that a little experimentation will give you a knowledge of its proper use. It is heartening to learn that some of our most modern cooks are beginning to use it again in rice, meat and fish dishes, and soup.

Please do not forget that cumin can be used as a small dwarf facer in your herb garden, as well as to impart demure beauty and fragrance to your borders. Cumin is an all-purpose herb. Look at one of the suggested herb garden plantings in Chapter 5 to see where cumin might best fit your plans. It is easy to grow and the only thing you will have to watch out for is to make sure the plants are not overrun by weeds.

DANDELION
*Taraxacum
officinale*
of the Compositae
family

The dandelion is a courageous little plant that has almost no peer for hardiness. Whether or not mankind agrees, it feels it has an important place among us and tries hard to please. It is one of the first to join us in the spring when many of its brothers and sisters stay covered and cosy until all signs of frost have disappeared. Its golden-yellow starlike blooms gleam forth like a reflection in the sea-green grass and its petals seem to say, 'Be of good cheer—spring is almost here'.

The dandelion plant will grow year after year from a deep, fleshy root and the deeply scalloped leaves grow in a low crown near the ground. They have admirable adaptability and can grow to a height of two or three feet to reach the sunlight, but will hug the ground if the lawn mower keeps them cut low. They say the only way to get rid of them is to poison them or to cut their roots. Many people do this. They still must have their place, however, because I have recently seen (with surprise and amusement) packets of dandelion seed displayed in the seed store near the grass seeds.

The dandelion is a native in Europe and Asia but is now common to temperate climates all over the world. It is a master at seed scattering, because each flower has a hundred and fifty or more little florets set in a cup and each floret is really a little flower. It has parts for growing and catching pollen, and the lower end produces a seed. When ripe, the seed 'builds' a feathery network, a pappus, on a stalk thinner than ♯60 thread. All of the pappi in the pappus make up what we know as a 'blowball', and the wind does the rest.

The Italians have always had a soft spot in their hearts for the dandelion, remembering that it is a first cousin to chicory, endive, and lettuce. They learned centuries ago that the secret of using dandelion to the palate's best advantage lay in the time of harvesting. The young leaves have a milky juice containing a pleasing bitterness that imparts that unusual something to a salad. If the leaves are young enough they can be used alone for salad greens. Even the roasted roots can be used as coffee.

DILL
Peucedanum graveolens
of the carrot family

With an oil so fragrant that some consider it to be the true anise of the Bible, dill is one of our oldest and most important herbs. It is native to the Mediterranean and Black Sea regions, although it was cultivated in Palestine in ancient times. Dill was very well known in Pliny's time and many writers of the Middle Ages extolled its virtues. It has been grown in the United States for about a hundred and fifty years and today most of our cultivation of the plant is done in California.

Dill makes a beautiful addition to any garden and is to be considered a 'must' for the herb gardener. It has smooth, hollow, branching stems that generally grow to a height of two to three feet and hold almost threadlike leaves. Numerous small yellow flowers appear in clusters around midsummer. Seeds are produced very freely and are flat in appearance. While the entire plant is extremely fragrant, the fragrant oils is in the seeds and they should be cleaned and dried with great care.

The dill seeds that are grown commercially do a creditable job but the fresh, home-cured seeds are even better. Another reason why the herb gardener should have dill high on his list is that the fragrant foliage loses much of its savour when dried. The fresh foliage can be harvested at any time.

Dill is famous the world over as a pickle ingredient, the largest single use for dill. It has been used for this purpose since the seventeenth century. In colonial days dill cakes were made for babies to chew on when they were teething because it purportedly had some soothing effect on the gums. It has been reported, too, that at one time dill was known as dilling or dulling because of its ability to soothe pain. It is, in fact, a remarkably effective reliever of stomach 'aches' arising from flatulence and is the active ingredient of Dill Water known to most mothers of babies.

Today there seems to be a growing interest in the use of the seeds, young leaves, and young stems for flavouring and seasoning a host of foods. The French have been the most ardent users of dill in cookery and they, of course, took the slight trouble to learn the specific 'know-how' of its use. Dill, with its wondrous bouquet (when used sparingly), would very probably have been used on a vastly larger scale in cookery had not most people overused it in their first experience with it. The fresh, chopped foliage is excellent with most meat and fish dishes. Another use that should be mentioned here is that of flavouring soaps. For this, the oil is extracted from the seeds.

It is suggested that you plant dill in your herb garden at least for its ornamental value and fragrance until time permits a little experimenting in the kitchen. Try the young, fresh leaves in soups, sauces, and salads, first with other established herb combinations known to you. Later it should be possible to get the most out of this very aromatic plant in your own way.

Seed should be sown early in the spring, preferably in warm sandy soil and in a place that will allow full sunshine. The plant does not seem to care particularly for transplanting. For other data on this subject, see Chapter 5.

FENNELS
Foeniculum
of the carrot family

While there are some minor differences among the three fennels, the most important attributes are common to all. As this is being written, a large plot of fennel is growing just outside the window. It is truly an inspiration to see its many divided leaflike structures, which give it an exquisite fernlike appearance. Here is a species native to southern Europe, although it was early found growing along all of the Mediterranean shores.

The fennels are really in the elegant class, since they possess all of the features required and desired by the herb gardener. These include fragrance and beauty in the garden, and by beauty we mean contrasting beauty that sets it apart from most of the other herbs but enables it to blend harmoniously with the over-all picture. The other features include the widespread uses for various parts of the fennel plant in cookery.

Since there are really three plants known generally as fennel, these are listed by their common names and botanical names as follows:

ORDINARY FENNEL (*Foeniculum vulgare*)—this is the common fennel of commerce that uses both the foliage and seeds for flavour. Common fennel will grow to a height of four to six feet.

SWEET FENNEL (*Foeniculum dulce*)—this is the one that is often called Florence fennel and even more often finochio. Sweet fennel, while in various characteristics very like ordinary fennel, grows only to about half the size of ordinary fennel. The fresh stalks of it are eaten to a large extent by Italians just as we eat fresh celery.

ITALIAN FENNEL (*Foeniculum vulgare piperitum*)—this is the one that is not too well known in the United States but apparently it is readily available in any Italian market. It is used primarily for its fresh stalks. This particular variety has also been called Sicilian fennel or carosella.

The fennels go so far back into history that we have no record of the beginning of their use. Certainly they were among the first herbs to be used. Along with some of the other well-known and widely used herbs, they deserve to be called classics because actually it took something of a classical nature to survive the many misuses that were tied in with the herbs of old.

For the herb gardener, the fennels are of the utmost importance. They have fragrance, flavour, beauty, and grace. They are delightfully and faintly anise-scented. Flower arrangers will find them very attractive, especially for church decorations.

There are some odd legends concerning fennel. Pliny said that before serpents cast off their old skins they ate fennel; he is also reported as saying that the juice of the fennel plant made the eyesight better; cures for cataracts on the eyes have been attributed to the roots of the fennel plant.

All of the fennels are easy to grow as annuals but they require a long growing season. The foliage of sweet fennel and the young stalks of carosella are extremely popular in salads and in the preparation of *hors d'oeuvres*.

In addition to the medicinal value of the various fennel seeds, discriminating cooks use the seeds in breads, cakes, and pastries of all sorts. They are also used in sauces, in many soups, as a flavour for teas and for more ardent drinks like wines and anisette. The fennels are truly remarkable herbs that every one should take advantage of.

FENNEL FLOWER
Nigella sativa
of the buttercup
family

The fennel flower is one of the loveliest of all flowers, yet it is so versatile that it is not commonly associated with beauty. Nature has done a tremendous job in handling all connected parts properly, in bringing out and maintaining its exotic beauty, which has been spoken of as 'youthful'! The chances are that it will remain, even unto its dried stage, exotic and beautiful.

The fennel flower is an Asiatic annual, welcomed by the horticulturist who is looking for the added touch of 'true blue' streaming blossoms for the garden and flower arrangements. To further enhance this effect, imagine how the featherlike foliage on the fennel flower would look with this blue stream. Flower arrangers cannot help being inspired by this combination. The plant grows to a height of ten or twelve inches, which contributes to its versatility. The feathery foliage is made of very finely chiselled leaves that are fragile, greatly resembling ferns, the basis for many church arrangements.

The fennel flower is among the oldest known herbs. Among the ancient Romans it was very highly esteemed in cookery and this accounts for one of its common names, Roman coriander. The fennel flower is said to be the 'Gith of Charlemagne' and the word comes from the Hebrew, *gesah*, which is mentioned in the Bible. Pliny makes frequent reference to it.

FEVERFEW
*Chrysanthemum
parthenium*
of the chrysanthe-
mum family

Fedderfew . . . feferfew . . . feberfew . . . and it was once supposed to be a valuable febrifuge, or abater of fever. Hence the name, which means to drive away. With its tender, torn, and jagged leaves and its double, white, miniature flowers full of pleasant pungence, feverfew is loved dearly by herb growers and is a 'must' for flower arrangers. The fact that it flowers all summer long is a great bonus to both groups. It makes an excellent background plant and will grow in almost any kind of soil.

Gerard says, 'It groweth in hedges, gardens, on old walls, it joyeth to grow among other odd places.' He also says, 'Feverfew is hot in the third degree and dry in the second, it clenseth, purgeth, and scoureth, and fully performeth all that bitter things can do. The fedderfew growing in my garden has a most pleasant flavour in respect of any of the rest.'

Feverfew is a native of Europe and today there are three well-known types: golden ball, lemon ball, and snow ball. The snow ball is especially lovely when used with roses for artistic arrangements. All three of these perennials dry beautifully for winter bouquets.

GARLIC
Allium sativum
of the lily family

There is nothing subtle about garlic. Even the most cursory thought of it evokes an almost overpowering flavour, a flavour that is not fleeting. That's garlic. It is thought by some that to chew a sprig of parsley after eating foods seasoned with it will remove its odour from the breath. But the honest garlic lover knows that nothing will remove the strength of garlic but time.

It is a hardy plant with broad leaves, a sister or brother of the onion and leek, all of the lily family. Garlic is a native of the south of Europe where it is used at mealtime just as freely as we use salt. Seasoning prepared from this herb comes from its pungent bulb, which is made up of many smaller bulbs called cloves. Many varieties are found, some with white buds and some with red cloves. There is one variety that is frequently called ramsons, the leaves of which are used by Europeans as we use spinach or as the French use sorrel. It is generally cooked in salted water containing butter and a generous sprinkling of pepper. Although the cook will consider that garlic's greatest contribution to mankind has been in putting the sparkle into food, it is probably the most valuable of medicinal herbs, protecting against infection, driving out catarrh and purifying the blood. Many today swear by its effectiveness in rheumatism.

Garlic can be an attractive addition to the kitchen herb garden with its showy dark green foliage and pink flowers. Bulbs can be set in

November and December or can be planted in the spring after all signs of frost have passed. Plant as you would plant onion sets. By late summer, when the tops are dry, take up the entire plant from the ground and dry thoroughly. Then separate cloves and remove the outer skin and all roots. It is best to store in a dry place. Garlic seems to have been put on earth for a purpose that is tied to our purse strings, because it can put zest into the dullest, ghostlike particle of food.

GERANIUM-SCENTED LEAVES of the geranium family

   Rose Geranium (*Pelargonium graveolens*)
   Lemon Geranium (*Pelargonium limonseum*)

These are widely different-looking plants. The apple, citron, lemon, nutmeg, peppermint, rose, and many others make up this highly select group of scented geranium leaves. The rose-and lemon-scented geraniums are the ones most used for making fragrant bouquets, flower arrangements, and potpourris. The leaves are also used to flavour jellies and puddings.

ROSE
GERANIUM
*Pelargonium
graveolens*

From the Cape of Good Hope came this one and it will grow as high as four feet in warm climates. Stems are literally stabbed to death with the many branches on it. The leaves, yellow-green in colour, are darker on top and lighter underneath. They are much divided, sub-divided, and have soft short hairs rough to the touch. The flowers really

57

steal the show with their lavender and pink hues that cannot be described.

LEMON
GERANIUM
*Pelargonium
limonseum*

The lemon geranium differs from the rose geranium in foliage pattern and flavour. Both reach upward about equally, and both are beautiful. The flowers are equally eye-pleasing and both bloom in June and July.

The rose- and lemon-scented geraniums are extremely ornamental when used as border plantings. For the cheerful and gay window box, these two will not fail you. For a fresh, clean scent and gay flowers, put a small arrangement on the breakfast table.

GERMANDER
*Teucrium
chamaedrys*
of the mint family

When growing this lovely perennial, you get the feeling that it is growing especially for you because it is the flower of our dreams and fills the gardens of our desires. I had the recent pleasure of visiting a lovely paved terrace and fenced-in herb garden. Completely surrounding the terrace was a border of germander. In the background bed were the taller herbs to complement the blue leather on the wrought-iron chairs. In planting boxes on each side of the kitchen door were chives, leeks, rocambole, and parsley for seasoning. On the wrought-iron-gate side were the sweet and fragrant rose and lemon geraniums. This quaint garden was truly an herb garden as it should be, but its focal point was the lush green border of germander. Gerard says, 'They floure and flourish from the end of May to the later end of August.' These flowers are reddish purple. The plant has many curved stems and grows to eighteen inches in height. Germander grows well in light sunny places in reasonably good soil and is used for ornamental borders. It has many uses in the field of medicine also.

Fragrance has been saved until the end here. It is magnificent, with undertones and overtones of other members of the mint family.

HOP
Humulus lupulus
of the Cannabinaceae
family

This fascinating plant never fails to bring back memories of my childhood in Virginia; one in particular is of a hop vine near the out-door kitchen of one of the old homes. Every time my parents took me to this place for a visit, my first stop was to say hello to my climbing friend with its pineapple-like cream-coloured flowers. Without fail, it would seem to be returning the greeting and at the same time trying to pretty itself up. At the dinner table it would always come to me—or at least part of it would—first as a flower bud in the salad; next in fragrant, crusty loaves of bread.

Gerard gives this interesting description of the hop: 'The Hop doth live and flourish by embracing and taking hold of poles, pearches, and other things upon which it climbeth. It bringeth forth very long stalkes, rough, and hairie; also rugged leaves like those of the Vine, or rather of Bryony, yet blackur and with fewer dented definitions; the floures hang downe by clusters from the tops of the branches, puffed up, set as it were with seales like little canes or sealed Pineapples of a whitish colour, tending to yellowness, strong of smell: the roots are slender and diversely folded one within the other.' He also made the remark: 'The hop joyeth in a fat and fruitful ground.' Pliny mentioned hops among the prickle plants. He said, 'They are more toothsome than nourishing, for they yield but very small nourishment.'

The hop vine is a native of northern temperate zones and today the lupulus species is widely grown commercially for brewing. Only the female flowers are useful for this purpose and they form, in pairs, the conelike body that contains the lupulin so valuable in brewing. The County of Kent is world famous for its hops and in the United

States, New York and Oregon are the chief growing centres. Tasmania, the Australian island state, contributes largely to the world supply and eighty-seven per cent of its production comes from one place, the Derwent Valley. Here harvesting begins around the first of March and continues for six weeks or more. Family units make a gala occasion out of stripping the cones from vines up to eighteen feet in height, laughing and joking and making the work seem like play. Lunchtime is like a picnic. After stripping, the cones are stuffed into burlap bags and taken to oasthouses or kilns for drying.

Medicinally the hop is a mild sedative and nerve nutrient much used to induce sleep for the over-active minded.

The hop vine would make an interesting conversation piece in any herb garden.

HOREHOUND
Marrubium vulgare
of the mint family

Horehound is a rare beauty in the herb garden—that is, for those who appreciate simple and uncomplicated lines and patterns. It should be a favourite with flower arrangers. When you look at the composite picture, the reasons become obvious.

The horehound plant pushes its way up to a height of about eighteen inches. It has very erect stems that are branchy and on these appear the toothed, greyish-green leaves, which are covered with a greyish-white down, smoother than velvet. The leaves are almost square and this should also excite the flower arranger's imagination. The plant bears beautiful white flowers in clusters that form whorls and spikes. The seeds are brown and have an oblong shape. It is a perennial, but a fresh sowing should be made after a few years, if at all possible, since the oil starts to lose quality as the plant becomes older. Seed should be sown in the early spring as soon as the soil can be worked. It does best in a poor soil and likes the sun. After it gets started, very little care is needed and no protection from cold weather need be given the horehound plant, as it is hardy. If the soil is too rich and moist, there will be less of the essential oil and it will be of poorer quality.

Horehound is one of the most unusual of the herbs still being used today in quantity in one way or another. It was widely used in cooking, though its use today in this field is limited to candies, used primarily for coughs and other mild respiratory ailments.

It has been with us for a long time, and there appears to be no let-up in the demand for its end-products, though it is not popular as it once was. Some of its past uses should be mentioned to demonstrate how popular it was years ago. A horehound drink was once made in Norfolk, England. Pliny said that it was a highly esteemed medicinal plant. Ancients believed that if it were put in milk and placed near flies it would kill them in one fell swoop. Long ago a snufflike material was made from the leaves. It was listed in Prince's catalogues in 1790, in Bartram's catalogue in 1814, and in the *American Herbal*, written by Stearns and published in 1801.

A popular author of many years ago listed the following recipe for horehound candy: 'To one pint of a strong decoction of the leaves and stems or the roots, add eight or ten pounds of sugar. Boil to candy "height" and pour into moulds or small paper cases previously well dusted with finely powdered lump sugar, or pour on dusted marble slabs and cut into squares.'

Bees are very partial to horehound nectar and a pleasant, top-quality honey is made from the flowers where they are abundant.

It should be used in minute quantities at first in conjunction with something sweet to buffer its bitterness. It is strange indeed that, with all the feeling against it, we still import sizeable amounts each year.

HORSE-RADISH
*Armoracia
rusticana*
of the mustard
family

Gerard says, 'Horse Radish brings forth great leaves, long, broad, sharpe pointed, and snipt about the edges, of a deepe greene colour like those of the great garden Dock (called of some, Monks Rubard, of others Patience), but longer and rougher. The stalk is slender and brittle, bearing at the top small white flowers; which being past, there follow small cods, wherein is the seed. The root is long and thick, white of colour, tast sharp, and very much biting the tongue like Mustard.' Gerard also has an interesting statement that refers to the tendency of horse-radish to spread: 'Divers thinke that this Horse Radish is an enemy to Vines and that the hatred between them is so great, that if the roots thereof be planted neere to the Vine, it bendeth backward from it, as not willing to have fellowship with it.'

Horse-radish is a native of the ancient oriental world and of south-eastern Europe, and while it is grown today for the large root only, it has been said that long before the roots were first used the leaves were cooked just as we cook collard greens.

For the discriminating gardener, Burpee says that horse-radish is easily grown in any good garden soil. One that is moist, fertile, deep, and medium heavy produces the largest and smoothest roots to grate for tender, pungent, stimulating flavour.

HYSSOP
Hyssopus
officinalis
of the mint family

Glamour and enchantment are built into the name 'hyssop'. There is still a tendency to hold the name almost in awe, for a number of reasons, one of which is frequent reference to it in biblical writings, even though scholars are convinced that the hyssop we know today is not the same. Enough confusions still surrounds the matter to add to the intrigue.

Hyssop is one of our oldest herbs from the standpoint of wide-spread use. Many famous ancient authors wrote about it romantically, medicinally, and culinarily. It is a beautiful evergreen native to the Mediterranean regions and was grown by the ancients and by medieval populations primarily for its use in medicine and to a lesser extent for its ornamental effect and use in cookery. Hyssop in most regions will grow to a height of eighteen to twenty-four inches. It has smooth stems; the terminal spikes contain the entire leaves and hold small clusters of blue flowers. There are also pink (or red) and white forms, but it might be advisable for the herb gardener to stick to the blue-flowered variety as it is supposed to be hardier. Here is one of the few herbs that seems to thrive best in partial shade; if the soils is too rich the plant will have a lush growth but the aromatic qualities drop off sharply. The seeds retain their viability for about three years. It is best to sow the seeds in early spring and transplant in early summer. If planting very much, sow the seed about six inches apart and in rows eighteen inches between.

Hyssop today is not used as extensively as in the past in cookery but this is due primarily to the vagaries of human nature and taste.

The stems, foliage, and flowers are all highly aromatic and have a hot, bitter taste, but it is this very bitterness of the oil that can enhance foods so much when used sparingly and adroitly. Almost everyone tends to use an overdose of herb seasonings, and this seems to be the case particularly with hyssop. The monks in Europe use the oil in flavouring sauces and soups. In some sections of Europe the oil is extracted commercially (one pound of oil from five hundred pounds of plant) and used in toilet article preparations.

You will enjoy hyssop in your herb garden and chances are great that, in addition to the fragrance and beauty you will enjoy outside, you will learn the artistry of using various parts of the plant in cookery, if you remember that a little bit goes a long, long way.

LAVENDER
Lavandula spica
of the mint family

At arms, each spikèd shrub doth stand
In couple-coloured gallantry,
Taught to submit before commands,
Yields now a soft perfumery.

JON BRADSHAW

Here are fragrance and beauty galore that are a part of almost every landscape design, whether it be around the house, in the flower garden, or in the herb garden. Lavender is one of the most wondrous products of nature. It has enjoyed a tremendous popularity down through the ages just for its fragrance and beauty, although at one time in the dim past it was put to the test in cookery, but to no avail.

E   65

It is a fairly hardy perennial that is native to the dry upland regions of southern Europe.

As to its appearance in the garden, compact clumps up to two and one half feet are formed and there are numerous erect stems with small grey leaves above which slender square flower stems arise. There is a multitude of violet-blue spiky flowers. Lavender does best in light, limey or chalky soil and it is well to remember that, if grown in rich soil, the plant grows larger but the flowers lack the very fragrance for which lavender is so famous.

There has been some confusion in the past in naming lavender. There are some who call *Lavandula vera* the true lavender. This same lavender has also been called *Lavandula officinalis*, *Lavandula angustifolia*, and *Lavandula spica*. All of the lavenders grow wild in the southern part of France, Spain, Italy, Corsica, and Sicily. There are, of course, many other varieties of lavender, which will not be mentioned here since it would only tend to add to the confusion that already exists.

Lavender with its fantastic history and background is a natural plant for legend. In this connection, it is said that in Tuscany lavender is used to protect little children from the evil eye, and in North Africa it is said that the Kabyle women believe lavender protects them from mistreatment by their husbands.

The name is derived from the Latin word *lavo*, which means to wash; a distillation of the flowers was used in ancient times to perfume water for washing the body. Today the United States alone imports over a quarter of a million pounds of oil of lavender each year, practically all of which goes into the preparation of toilet waters. The oil is distilled from fresh flowers, the most aromatic part of the plant. Since the entire plant contains the oil, the scent of lavender grown in the garden can be preserved simply by drying the young foliage and flowering tops. The best of all lavender perfumes are made in England, where the oil is extracted from cultivated plants. In France the oil is distilled from wild plants. It is thought that *Lavandula vera* produces the best oil for perfumery. An interesting aspect of the use of lavender in perfumery is the fact that, the deeper the colour of the calyx, the stronger the fragrance. It is said that the yield of oil from sixty flowering spikes of lavender amounts to only one ounce and in England, where the best oil is produced, it is said that twenty-five pounds of oil can be expected from one acre of cultivated plants.

The word 'lavender' seems to me to encompass all of the things we know about the plant: lavender means fresh, lovely, lasting, fragrant scent for the herb garden, beauty that is almost awe-inspiring, and flower-fresh linens, sachets, potpourris, and nosegays.

LEEK
Allium porrum
of the lily family

To tender palates and taste buds, leek is more pleasing than onion. It is one of the milder members of the lily family and it is for this very mildness that leek is growing more and more toward king-size stature in the field of cookery.

It originated in central Asia, followed by cultivation in western Asia and Mediterranean lands. It is mentioned frequently in the Bible, which states how, during the wanderings of the Israelites in the wilderness, they longed for the onion, leek, and garlic they had had in Egypt. It has been in common use all over Europe for as long as there is a record of plants, and by 1775 leek was in cultivation by the native Indians and early colonists of America.

The name comes from the Anglo-Saxon word *leac;* the Romans called it *porrum,* and they considered that the best leeks came from Egypt. Nero had a tremendous appetite for leek and it is said that he was named *porrophagus* because of it. Strangely enough, Nero was of the opinion that leek improved his voice. Leek is so famous that it is the national emblem of Wales. There was a time in the Middle Ages when leek and garlic both were more popular than the onion, but now, of course, the reverse is true.

The stems of the leek generally grow to a height of two to two and one half feet. They are flat and solid as compared to those of the onion, which are round and hollow. Like the onion, took, leek forms a true bulb and in one reliable reference book it is described as having a bulbous, cylindrical root and long, broad succulent leaves. It likes a rich soil containing plenty of humus, and while it can be grown from a seed bed with later transplanting, it is more easily grown from young bulbs or 'sets'.

The bulb and the base, which is usually blanched by having soil heaped about it continually, are the parts of leek used in salads and to give a wonderful flavour to stews. It can be used to great advantage in anything for which onion flavour is a bit too strong. In fact many people have become so accustomed to the milder flavour of leek that they do not think in terms of onion any more. Now it is leek and more leek.

For those who may be interested, there is a wild leek, an American plant known as *Allium tricoccum.*

LEMON
VERBENA
Lippia citriodora
of the Verbena
family

Lemon verbena, unlike most of the other herbs, is not a hardy plant and cannot stand cold winters. It has so much to offer, however, that it is still worth while to have even in the colder areas of the country where it will be necessary to transplant it from the ground to a pot or a small tub during the months of frost and snow. From Virginia south, there seems to be no need for such protection.

Lemon verbena is a native of the Argentine, Chile, and Peru. It first reached Europe in 1784 and has become naturalized there, especially in the southern portions. It is also grown in many other sections of the world, such as India and South Africa.

The plant is unusual in its over-all appearance. The stems are woody and branching with a slight downy effect and in places one will find marks of red. The leaves are pointed, light yellow-green in colour, with an oblong shape, very shiny above and dull below. The underside is rough to the touch. It is such a fragrant plant that, when brushed against even slightly, an odour of lemon emanates from it. It has a very long blooming season and you will find flowers in both summer and autumn. They are small and arranged in spikes with colours of white and purple intermixed. Some have said that they are not especially decorative but they are pleasant to look at. The plant is one of the tallest herbs, at times growing to a height of as much as ten feet, although in most cases it averages from four to six feet in height.

Because of the nature of the plant, lemon verbena is commonly thought of as a pot plant and is grown primarily for its fine and delicate lemon fragrance. However, it does have some culinary value in teas and fruit drinks. Oils extracted from the leaves are also used in perfumery.

LOVAGE
Ligusticum
officinale
of the carrot family

Lovage was one of the first 'wonder drugs', according to John Gerard's *Herball*. Its use today, however, is primarily in the confectionery field, where the young stems are handled like those of angelica; these candied stems are delightful.

Lovage is an unusual-looking plant that could be the conversation piece of your herb garden. It is a hardy perennial and native to the Mediterranean region. It has dark green shining leaves with a 'different' look about them, usually divided into two or three segments. Close to the top, the hollow, erect stems divide to form whorled branches on which appear bundles of beautiful yellow flowers during the blooming season. The fruits (or seeds) are hollow and highly aromatic. The leaves are an excellent ingredient of salads.

Seeds can be planted in either autumn or spring and preferably in rich moist soil. You can look at one of the suggested landscape patterns in Chapter 5 to see how and where lovage will fit into your plans for the future. There are still many culinary delights locked in the 'safe for exciting tastes', waiting for someone to discover the right combination. You may be that person.

POT
MARIGOLD
Calendula officinalis
of the Compositae
family

This gem of the garden is considered by some the showiest and most decorative plant in the herb garden. Its beauty is so outstanding that it is in a class by itself. Growing to a height of twelve to eighteen inches, the plant has graceful lines, sweetness, and spiciness.

The pot marigold is native to Asia and southern Europe but has grown in this country since the time of the earliest settlers. Its stems are furry, deep dark green, and many-leaved. The leaves are soft and long, sometimes reaching six inches in length. The flowers put on a dazzling show, with blossoms opening all summer long and most abundant in the fall, long after the first frosts. The blossoms are yellow and orange, with round flat tops, and they are velvety to the touch. Many rows of ray florets, some yellow and some deep orange, surround the ones making up the centre disc, and—most unusual—they have no scent. This tender annual grows readily from seed if you wait until warm weather has definitely arrived before sowing. Two sowings can be made in most sections, one in the spring and one about July the first, so that two harvests can be made.

Uses for the pot marigold include seasoning, colouring for butter, and a replacement for saffron. There are some who claim that it has no flavour, since it has no scent, while others claim that it has flavour if you know how to use it and even go so far as to claim that the tastiest marigolds are those with the deepest orange colour.

MARJORAMS of the mint family

Sweet Marjoram (*Marjorana hortensis* or *Origanum marjorana*)
Pot Marjoram (*Origanum vulgaris*)

SWEET
MARJORAM
Marjorana hortensis
or
Origanum marjorana

Of all herbs that have been known to date, sweet marjoram is near the top of the popularity list. It is probably the most popular of all savouries and there are innumerable recipes that call for its use. In addition, it is certainly one of the most fragrant herbs to have in the garden. The plant is extremely attractive, being of dainty texture, as smooth as velvet, and having tiny green balls hanging from the stems like ornaments on a Christmas tree. The flowers come from these tiny balls.

Sweet marjoram is native to the Mediterranean region and has been known and used for many centuries. In the warmer climates it grows as a perennial, but because of its inability to cope with frost and snow, it has to be grown as an annual in the colder climates. At various times through the ages sweet marjoram has been acclaimed for almost every imaginable use in the fields of beauty, fragrance, flavour, and medicine. At one time it was thought that it had the power to keep fresh milk sweet, which accounts for the first part of the name 'sweet marjoram'. Many legends are connected with sweet marjoram. On the isle of Crete it was the symbol of honour, and it has been reported that at one time in Sicily it was thought to possess the gift of banishing sadness. In India it is said to be sacred to Siva and Vishnu. Having survived many centuries of medicinal testing, sweet marjoram has found its widest acceptance as an important cooking aid.

When one is close to nature and its complex 'simplicity', it seems natural to think of it as being made up of billions of manufacturing plants. In the case of the herbs, each one is a tiny manufacturing plant specializing in the production of oils that we call essential oils. These oils determine the use and acceptability of the herbs, and the essential oil in sweet marjoram is one of nature's finest. It has a host of uses, including some in medicine and others in perfumery, toilet preparations, and soaps.

As far as the herb gardener is concerned, it is the leaf of the sweet marjoram plant that is of the greatest importance. When the leaves are fresh, their fragrance and flavour are an unusual combination of sharpness and pleasant aromatic bitterness, with perhaps an overtone of camphor. Dried leaves are more subdued and the fragrance and flavour are more reminiscent of perfume.

There is scarcely a more colourful herb to add beauty to any garden. The main stem of the plant is a brownish purple in most areas, while the side branches have a reddish tint. These stems will normally grow to a height of twelve inches. The leaves are really the most beautiful part of the plant, since they are soft-textured, greenish grey in colour, rather small, and covered with a beautiful down. The flowers are rather inconspicuous but also present a most unusual appearance. They are white or cream in colour and seem to creep out a leaf one at a time from a container that might be likened to a sea shell or a cocoon.

The culinary uses of sweet marjoram are so numerous that they cannot be listed here singly but it is the perfect seasoning for chicken and turkey stuffings, and mushrooms taste very different when cooked with the right amount of sweet marjoram. Many people who find sage, our most widely used herb today, a little too flavourful for them turn to sweet marjoram for poultry stuffing. Recently I learned about its use in sweet fritters made with spinach in Italy. It is also an excellent garnish for salads and is very good when used as a salad green.

Sweet marjoram, either alone or with other herbs and spices, is widely utilized by food producers.

No herb garden should be without sweet marjoram. You will

find that it is ideal as a facer plant for any semiformal or informal garden. It is also ideal as a border plant or edging. Once you are accustomed to the wondrous delights of sweet marjoram, you will find that a larger space than anticipated will be needed to grow it.

POT
MARJORAM
Origanum vulgaris

This plant is often referred to as wild marjoram. It is a true perennial and a native of Europe. Although sweet marjoram seems to have been in the spotlight for centuries, pot marjoram was probably known and used for quite some time before sweet marjoram came on the scene.

It has gone through all of the trials and tribulations suffered by other widely used, well-known herbs and seems to have survived in good fashion. At one time it was used or at least tried for just about every imaginable dish and ailment. Pliny wrote at great length on its medicinal uses. Today, pot marjoram finds its widest use in Latin-American soups, vegetables, and meats. One important feature of pot marjoram should be remembered at all times by the cook: the fragrant oil in the leaves of pot marjoram is very strong-tasting and therefore must be used sparingly and with discrimination. Gradually you will develop a subtle knowledge of it.

The plant is a pleasing one that grows to a height of two to two and one half feet, has an abundance of aromatic leaves, and in July bears flowers in flat-topped clusters that have a pink to purplish tint. Pot marjoram lends itself to indoor growing, and is especially pretty in the kitchen window box or as a potted herb.

AMERICAN MANDRAKE
or
MAY APPLE
*Podophyllum
peltatum*
of the barberry
family

It is an unusual plant in many respects and has stood in high esteem since ancient times. It should fill a shady corner in your herb garden or an especially cool, moist place in the wild-flower garden.

The shield-shaped leaves and single white cuplike flower make it an interesting plant to watch. The umbrellalike leaves are said to unfurl only during April showers, as if to protect its lovely white blossoms. In July it bears a sweet, many-sided fruit resembling a lemon. It has been known as the mandrake and wild lemon, but without a doubt the name 'May apple' fits it best. May apple grows to a height of about one to one and one half feet and its leaves sometimes measure twelve inches across. The leaves are on flowerless stems, coming from separate rootstock, and are a dark green above and a light green below. The fruit generally measures about two inches in length. This is the only edible part of the plant.

The sweet fruit has been used for making preserves, just as we use the ground cherry. An old formula for the mild May apple was to boil slowly with peppers and other hot spices.

Pioneers and woodsmen found the fruit refreshing but were warned against eating any other part of the plant. They were asked to mark well the locations where the plants grew for the qualified herbalist, as their virtues were many in the field of medicine.

Strange effects are supposed to be inherent in the May apple, or mandragora, later to be called mandrake. In biblical times Rachel desired philters made from the ground dried roots of this loved plant, which resembled the male and female form. It was said to cause women to be fruitful and bear children. We are told that young Reuben, son of Leah, brought home the plants for their beauty and the fruits for

74

the sake of their sweet smell. There is a legend that says May apple is to be found only in the shadow of the gallows, or where a life has been lost. It was supposed to spring up in profusion to restore vigour, or help to maintain life. This must have been one of the reasons why John Bartram called Virginia a 'Garden of Eden', on his trek through the virgin territory, which was filled with the wonderful bounties of nature.

The ancients knew the plant well from the Mediterranean region. It is found more generally in the Blue Ridge and Appalachian Mountains. The May apple is said to be found as far south as the Gulf of Mexico and west into Minnesota and Texas in the United States of America.

MINTS of the mint family

> Peppermint (*Mentha piperita*)
> Spearmint (*Mentha viridis*)
> Apple Mint (*Mentha rotundifolia*)

The mint bed is an essential part of all country house gardens where culinary herbs are as important as vegetables in the kitchen garden. Peppermint, spearmint, and apple mint are grouped together here because they make up a compatible mint bed. They are grown this way in my herb garden; they are also among the most widely used members of the important mint family.

PEPPERMINT
Mentha piperita

Peppermint is native to Europe and has been naturalized in the United States to such an extent that it will grow well in almost any moist garden. This plant should be included in a mint bed because it possesses fragrance, flavour, and beauty. Its fragrance is more delicate than that of spearmint because the menthol present in the peppermint plant, the main constituent found in oil of peppermint, is responsible for the more cooling and stimulating flavour. The plant is a handsome one, with branching stems up to three feet in length which do not stand erect but curve outward. The stems are on the reddish side and the tips are often entirely red. The leaves are a deep green, numerous, spear-shaped, and have toothed edges. Cylindrical spikes of beautiful rosy lavender flowers appear toward the end of July and remain through August.

With its great importance since the earliest days of recorded history, it is natural that ancient scholars should have described mint. Many unusual claims were made for it. Pliny said that mint stimulates the brain and therefore students should wear a crown of mint while studying. He also advised sprinkling the room with vervain water, to make guests merry at a dinner party, because in the language of flowers the vervain signifies 'enchantment'.

Peppermint is important commercially as the source of oil of peppermint, which is distilled from the plants. Plucked from the mint bed, the leaves will give you an almost endless source of pleasant coolness in almost any beverage, including plain water. In flavour and fragrance, it dominates all other herbs used as teas. Peppermint tea is good either hot or iced; it should not be made too strong. A hot cup of tea in the middle of the afternoon, together with a few crisp gingersnaps, is very refreshing.

SPEARMINT
Mentha viridis

If there is to be a mint bed, then there must be spearmint. This is the mint that makes the kitchen more fragrant and full of flavour. A native of Europe, it has often been referred to as curly-leaf mint. It is a little lower growing than peppermint and is a more compact plant. The stems, like those of peppermint, curve outwards and do not stand erect. The leaves are smaller than *Mentha piperita,* more crinkly and tend to fold up within themselves. They are in opposite pairs and the edges are indented to give a pointed effect. The flowers are off-white and generally arrive late in July.

The spearmint plant is also important commercially. The extracted oil is used to flavour chewing gums, soaps, and dental preparations. It is best known in the kitchen, where it is used in a host of ways. No cook needs to be reminded of its value in UNIVERSAL MINT SAUCE for the traditional leg of lamb, in drinks, and in salads. It is also very popular for fruit cups, various confections, and french dressing for a macedoine of fruit. Many prefer it in iced beverages. It goes well with dainty sandwiches.

Another pleasing feature of the spearmint plant is that when it is dried it has tints and tones of red and bronze and can be used nicely for winter arrangements in copper containers.

APPLE
MINT
*Mentha
rotundifolia*

There are many other well-known members of the mint family, but apple mint has been selected because it illustrates a different portion of the over-all mint picture. Apple mint blends, in a most unusual way, fragrance and flavour reminiscent of all that is good in fruit, with the mellowness of the apple and overtones of pleasant mintiness. It is a beautiful plant that will generally grow to a height of eighteen inches. It is a soft plant, with more down on the stems than on the leaves, which are greenly cool in appearance. It has lovely creamy flower spikes. One of the most attractive features of apple mint is that the erect stems are not crowded with leaves. For the flower arranger it could be a real gem in the soft lustre of pewter containers.

MUSTARDS of the Cruciferae family

> Black or Brown Mustard (*Sinapis nigra*)
> White or Yellow Mustard (*Sinapis alba*)

Mustard has been known to man since prehistoric times, long before anyone discovered that the addition of either turmeric or saffron to prepared mustard gives it that very eye-appealing yellow colour and delightful flavour. So people then must have eaten mustards that we probably would not look at a second time.

Jesus mentioned mustard at least twice: 'If ye have faith as a grain of mustard seed, ye shall say unto this mountain, remove hence unto yonder place and it shall remove.' He also said, 'The kingdom of God . . . is like a grain of mustard seed.'

BLACK OR
BROWN
MUSTARD
Sinapis nigra
of the Cruciferae
family

The black or brown mustard with its tall-growing stalks (sometimes up to four feet high) and small yellow flowers was used in medieval times in concocting love potions, but long before that Pliny had recommended it 'to overcome lassitude in females'.

WHITE OR
YELLOW
MUSTARD
Sinapis alba
of the Cruciferae
family

The white mustard is the one so much used in the herb garden for its young foliage, which as always been a favourite for salads.

Mustard originally came from Europe and southwestern Asia. Today we grow large quantities of it in this country and import the rest of our supply from Canada, Denmark, the United Kingdom, and the Netherlands.

Prepared mustard, as we know it now, is a comparatively recent thing, according to one writer. It was first mixed a few hundred years ago by a woman in Durham, from the ground seeds of wild mustard.

NASTURTIUM
Tropaeolum minus
of the Tropaeolum
family

Think for a while about those herbs that are most precious to you. Wouldn't you be apt to put the generous nasturtium at the top of the list? It offers much in ways that have seldom been equalled. If there is to be a garden at all, whether it be a flower garden or an herb garden, there must be nasturtium. It can be called one of the classic herbs, for it fulfils the requirements of any gardener: it has fragrance and beauty in the garden and fragrance and flavour in the kitchen. These are the true measuring sticks that determine whether or not an herb belongs in the select classical group.

Coming originally from the Andes of Peru where only pure, clean, soft air prevailed, this annual fills the surrounding atmosphere with a fragrance so magnificently elegant and penetrating that its name, 'nasturtium', describes its ability to make the nostril quiver and twist: from the words *nasus* (nose) and *torquere* (to twist) came nasturtium, the 'nose twister'.

Wherever you find a temperate climate you will find the nasturtium. There are two types: *Tropaeolum majus*, which grows very tall, and *Tropaeolum minus*, the low-growing, less space-taking, more abundantly flowering type. It is the latter one that is described here. It grows to a height of twelve inches normally, with leaves that tend to be round, smooth, and lighter green underneath than on top. It has very conspicuous flowers that range in colour from yellow through orange to dark red. The entire plant is covered lightly with down and gives off a spicy fragrance.

The nasturtium is so easily grown that nothing special need be said here, except that if you use soil that is too rich you will have mostly foliage and very few buds and blossoms! You will find very simple growing instructions on the Growing Charts in Chapter 5.

The flowers are so eye-pleasing that one tends to lose sight of the many culinary uses for the foliage, seeds, flowers, buds, and pods. Everything but the root is used in the culinary field. The young tender stems and leaves are extremely succulent in salads, the chopped young leaves are very tasty in sandwiches, the blossoms enhance fruit salads, and minced blossoms can be blended into creamed butter or cheese for use as a spread. The unripe and still green seeds with their peppery taste are the zestful part of the plant and are used as substitutes for the exotically flavoured capers. The unopened flower buds are peppery like the seeds and find wide use in many dishes. Try a single seed in a cup of tea for a real taste thrill!

ORÉGANO
Origanum vulgare
virens
of the mint family

This is the merry herb of old Spain that has a hot, biting taste but a sweet smell. It is a native of the Mediterranean area and has been naturalized in Britain. Orégano is the Spanish name for marjoram— though the flavour is stronger and has a pleasantly bitter undertone.

Gerard said this about organy (as he spelled it): 'These plants grow wild in Spaine, Italy, and other hot countries. The first of these I found growing in divers and Chalky fields and high-waies neere unto Sittingburne and Rochester in Kent, and also neere unto Cobham House and Southfleet in the same country.' It has been said that in Pliny's time orégano was known as the 'joy of the mountain' or 'goates marjoram'.

It has lavender clustered flower heads that bloom in August and deep green leaves that dry to a lovely light green colour. This perennial generally will grow to a height of eighteen to twenty-four inches. Italy, France, Greece, Chile, and Mexico export the dried leaves. It is also available in crushed and ground forms.

Orégano should be numbered among the many other wonderful spices on our shelves and used in tomato dishes, mushroom dishes, with beef, lamb, pork, and chicken. It is also used in soups, sauces, and French dressing. You will find additional uses for orégano in the Herb Chart on page 118.

PARSLEY
Petroselinum sativum
(or *crispum*)
of the Umbelliferae
or carrot family

This is one of the oldest known herbs and records indicate that it has been under cultivation for at least two thousand years. It is native to the Mediterranean; Bartram, in his *American Herbal*, stated that it came to the Americas in the seventeenth century. Theophrastus described both the crowded, dense, curly-leaf type and the open-growing type as early as the fourth century. During the first century the Romans were familiar with the plain and curled types. They wore parsley in chaplets around their necks to ward off intoxication. Both Greeks and Romans knew it well for its fresh fragrant beauty as a garnish and for its wonderful flavour. It is probably the best known of all the herbs. This is borne out by the fact that it has long received endorsement from the gardening world and history and legend are full of stories about this ancient plant.

Parsley is easily grown and no kitchen garden should be without it. The flat-leaved varieties are known to contain more vitamins and iron than the curly-leaved types, but for beautiful garnishing and exotic edging for herb borders, I recommend the Emerald, sometimes called the curled dwarf, because it is a frilly queen in the garden. Since the seeds are very slow to germinate, I have successfully mixed parsley and radish seeds and sown them in the radish bed. As the radishes grow, they will shade the soil and help the little parsley plants to get started. After the radishes have been harvested, the parsley will not have to be thinned out.

Parsley has many uses, not only for garnishes, but for soups, stews, sauces, salads, and on and on. Don't forget to chew a sprig of parsley after eating food seasoned with garlic so you will be more acceptable to your friends! The garlic addict cannot expect it to be completely effective, but it can sweeten the breath of the moderate garlic eater. But remember also to take every possible advantage of the many uses of health-giving parsley, whether or not you eat garlic.

PENNYROYAL
Mentha pulegium
of the mint family

Whether it's pennie royall, pudding grass, or pennyroyal, here is royalty . . . although one does not generally associate a penny with royalty. Here is royalty that loves the hillsides, and the sunny roadsides, and the meadows. Pennyroyal also loves moist creek banks—hardly the natural habitats of a prince, but certainly those of a roaming vagabond prince. And what a merry prince he is! He is actually a native of Europe and portions of Asia but now has become a good-will ambassador with the world for his domain. He roams about, generally acting himself, but at other times disguised as a dusty beggar or a country urchin . . . and in fact he has been called an urchin by some unknowing people. He seems to prefer anonymity, seldom calling attention to himself . . . yet he is most certainly a part of the herb picture.

Pennyroyal has square prostrate stems that will readily take root at the nodes; these stems bear greyish-green, almost round leaves. The slightly hairy or fuzzy leaves hold whorled clusters of little lilac-blue flowers, which rise in tiers, one above the other, at the nodes. They bloom from June to August.

As I mentioned earlier, my father was a timber surveyor and contractor, and itinerant timbermen and lumberjacks of many nationalities were always coming from and going to places all over the globe. One of my earliest memories is of how they gathered the merry little pennyroyal to put into their straw ticks (mattresses for their beds), which had been made from new-harvested straw. I remember that they also scattered it all over the floors of their bunk-houses to keep fleas away. We have used it in recent years in straw beds for our collie dogs and found that it does repel fleas.

Pennyroyal is yours for many uses. When horseback riding with our father, he would have us put bunches of pennyroyal in the bridles of our horses to keep flies from annoying them, he also had us crush the leaves in our hands and then rub our faces to keep the gnats from biting when we went fishing with him. Remember that it is the small mint in the garden, is a fairly hardy perennial, and has been cultivated commercially in Europe for the high-quality aromatic oil that it yields. At one time twelve pounds of oil per acre of pennyroyal was considered a good yield. Although peppermint and spearmint seem to have a pleasanter flavour, pennyroyal can also contribute to foods and beverages when used sparingly. The leaves, green or dried, have gone into many tasty puddings and sauces prepared by our ancestors in days long past. They could still if only the gardeners, especially the junior gardeners, would cultivate the acquaintance of this aromatic prince of the mint family. Prince or urchin, it matters not, pennyroyal has been with us a long, long time . . . and we hope that he will be around for a much longer time.

PEPPER
TABASCO
Capsicum
frutescens
of the potato family

Here is the hottest of all peppers! It is so hot that it seems as though the seed and plant cannot get the hotness out of their systems quickly enough . . . because they bear fruit prolifically, and the fruit does not grow on the stem of the plant but nearly erect on the branches so that it can be easily gathered. Once off the plant, this pepper tabasco holds its own against the world with no trouble whatsoever. 'Tabasco' is a Mexican word meaning 'land where the soil is humid'. Cortez stopped at Tabasco on his way to Mexico for the first time. It was there that he saw the Mayans using the small, red, hot peppers with such apparent delight. Woe to the unfortunate person who does not know that these peppers must be partaken of sparingly!

SMALL RED CHILI PEPPER
Capsicum annuum

There is one more pepper that must be included here—the small red chili pepper. This plant is very erect and quite bushy, and the bright red fruit is about one and one half inches long, in the form of a cone. This pepper plant with its bright red would add highlights to any herb garden. It is used in pepper sauce and in pickling. Pepper tabasco and the small red chili can be grown in temperate climates. We have them growing in our herb garden.

POPPY
Papaver somniferum
of the Papaveraceae
or poppy family

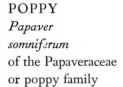

The opium poppy is our subject here, and though it does not quite measure up to the ultimate in beauty found in the oriental poppy, it is a showy plant with a rather quiet beauty all its own. It is a native of the Mediterranean area but has been naturalized in the United States.

The plant must be described from two separate and distinct points of view or, rather, two architectural and social planes. One view shows a beautiful grey-green plant that has been known to rise to a height of four feet, although it will be found mostly in the two- to three-foot range. It reaches upward on stems that are bluish-green and stand proudly erect. It is not a many-leaved plant, which fact contributes greatly to the effect of simplicity, but there are enough leaves to add a long whorl of greyish-green colour at regular intervals, and these become shorter and shorter as they ascend the stem. The opium poppy unfolds its delicate white flowers with a ballet-like grace—at times they are tinted with pinkish-purple flowing lines. The blooming period is in July and lasts for only a few short days. The pods are about two inches long and one inch wide and they seem to be trying to explode with their valuable cargo of tiny brownish-black seeds. The other view is quite opposite in effect. In brief, the opium poppy is the source of opium, morphine, codeine, and heroin, and though these are used as medicines, they have also been greatly misused—to such an extent that they have probably caused more degradation and misery than the products of any other plant.

Much lore surrounds the opium poppy. Pliny said that a decoction of poppy seeds, honey, and wine was served as a second course on the tables of the ancients. It appears to have been used as a narcotic since the earliest days.

The seeds from the opium poppy are free of any drug and are widely used as a topping for rolls, breads, cakes, cookies, and pastries, or as a filling for cakes, coffee-cakes, and pastries. Try the seeds in noodles and salads: a new taste thrill is yours for the asking. The seeds themselves have a pleasant, crunchy, nutlike flavour. In southern Europe, olive oil is often adulterated with an oil found in the seeds from a dark variety of the opium poppy.

The plant is easily grown and you will find simple instructions for growing on a chart in Chapter 5. In the United States and Great Britain a permit must be obtained for the growing of the opium poppy or any species or variety of poppy from which opium can be extracted. The narcotic is derived from the scrapings from the seed pod. The poppy petals are used for wrapping the opium. The fact that you must have a permit should not discourage you from including this very attractive plant in your herb garden.

RHUBARB
Rheum rhaponticum
of the Polygonaceae
family

This true rhubarb of the ancients has literally travelled around the world from the Mediterranean and Asia Minor. It is an aristocrat of nature's wonderful herbs.

Gerard devotes three full pages to the description and illustration of the various rhubarbs. He also describes many virtues of this plant. One of these reads: 'Mesues saith that Rhubarb is a harmless medicine, and good at all times, and for all ages, and likewise for little children and women with child.'

For a variety of colour and form in the herb garden, the new brilliant red rhubarb, which grows only from divisions, should be cultivated. When one stalk is cut, another fills in to take its place. It has an unusual loveliness in flower arrangements and its very colourful stalks and emerald-green leaves create a matchless and sparkling contrast in the arrangement. It is also the sweetest rhubarb you have ever tasted and does not lose its colour in cooking. You will find it to be excellent in sauces, pies, and parfaits. Use only the stalk, as the leaves are toxic. Three plants are enough for the average family to grow. It is eye-catching and ornamental for its mass forms in the herb garden.

ROCAMBOLE
Allium
scorodoprasum
of the Liliaceae or
lily family

Rocambole sounds like the name of a new Latin-American dance step. Most of the Latin-American rhythms subconsciously remind us of almost everything we have ever associated with the good things in life. Rocambole is not a dance step, but a herb which exhilarates the taste buds. It is sometimes known as the giant garlic, and was first grown in Asia Minor and southeastern Europe. It is very closely related to garlic and should be to garlic what leek is to onion. It is milder and more delectable than garlic. Hence, it finds favour with those people who prefer a subtler and more subdued fragrance and flavour than garlic.

The plant's appearance seems to reflect both humorous clownishness and architectural greatness on the move. The stems look like huge shock-absorber springs and they go through peculiar gyrations before starting to stand erect. On top are hidden flowers that eventually become bulbils. These are the rocambole cloves, which are used just as garlic cloves are.

Rocambole has more bonuses to offer than most of its relatives of the lily family. During the summer its brightest of bright green leaves slip into quiet slumber for a short period of time, after which new leaf growth starts. These young leaves are tender and mild and will certainly help to make your salads tastier if you use them lightly!

LESSER-
LEAVED GARLIC

Rocambole scordoprasum minus is sometimes called rockenbollen because it grows among rye (*rocken* for rye and *bolle* for a bulb). It is much smaller than the giant mentioned above. Its long slender bulbs are wrapped in brownish skins, the flowers and stems have daintier proportions. It is sometimes called the European leek, but it is best known as a lesser-leaved garlic.

ROSEMARY
Rosmarinus
officinalis
of the mint family

No other herb is quite as close to our hearts as rosemary. The rocky coasts of France and Spain were its home originally. Pliny gave it the name of *rosmarinus*, which means sea dew. Rosemary with its lacy foliage is a magnificent gem in the garden for its haunting yet ever-present spiky sweetness. The extraordinarily beautiful fragrance comes from an oil that is extracted on a tremendous scale in Europe by manufacturers of eau-de-Cologne. This world-renowned fragrance comes not only from the flowers but from the foliage as well. In most rosemary areas many women store the leaves throughout the long winter months because they seem to keep the surrounding air fragrantly alive, carrying a breath of spring on every dreary day.

Rosemary is a favourite of the flower arranger and also of discriminating people who can appreciate its use with culinary delights that are nearly bouquet complete but need that special little blessing to raise them above the ordinary.

This is an invaluable addition to any herb garden. Besides the uses mentioned for the kitchen, it is a very ornamental plant. After the plant has started to mature, it develops tiny leaves that are as grey as a tropical Spanish moss. There is a lovely legend about rosemary: the Virgin Mary spread her linen over a white-flowered bush of rosemary and ever after the flowers were as blue as her own robe.

ROSES of the rose family

>Damask rose (*Rosa damascena*)
>Provence rose (*Rosa gallica*)
>Eglantine (*Rosa eglanteria*)

Shakespeare said: 'The summer's flower is to the summer sweet.' Very probably William Shakespeare had in mind two and possibly all three of these when those lines were written; and he must have been a real prophet and lover of fragrance and beauty. These are the three oldest roses in cultivation. They are considered to be the most fragrant roses in the world and have long been the basis for many perfumes.

DAMASK ROSE
Rosa damascena

The damask rose is a native of southeastern Europe, where it has been used for centuries in making attar of roses. It is second only to the cabbage rose in the strength of its perfume. It is a hardy shrub and once planted, is very easily maintained. The flower is a pale pink, thin-textured, and semi-double. The blooming period comes generally sometime between the middle of June and the middle of July and lasts only ten days. The greatest fragrance comes from dried flowers and stems. In obtaining the damask rose for your herb garden, it is very important that you specify the botanical name *Rosa damascena,* since there are some other forms that are similar and some are even misnamed in old catalogues.

PROVENCE ROSE
Rosa gallica

The Provence rose is often called the French rose and, like the damask rose, has long been one of the sources of attar of roses. It can be grown in your herb garden just as you grow the damask. It is a hardy plant and requires very little maintenance, once planted. The flower is a deep reddish-rose colour, semi-double with approximately fifteen petals. Again, the fragrance increases after the stems and petals have been dried. And again, when ordering the Provence rose for your garden, it is very important that you specify the botanical name *Rosa gallica,* to avoid the possibility of obtaining one of many other forms developed from the true Provence rose.

EGLANTINE
Rosa eglanteria

The eglantine is often called sweetbriar. It, like the damask and Provence roses, is and has been for ages a source of attar of roses, so widely used in perfumes. It is also easily grown and requires very little maintenance, once started. The eglantine or sweetbriar has a colour that is very similar to mauve. The flowers are double and so fragrant that they seem to be straight out of the heavens. In *Cymbeline,* Shakespeare mentioned a low hedge of apple-scented eglantine. It of course is a shrub like the damask and Provence and is treelike in growth. It has an unusual type of fruit that is long like an olive, and stone red when ripe, downy within. This part is rich in vitamins. Gerard said, 'The fruit when it is ripe maketh most pleasant meats and banqueting dishes, as tarts and suchlike; the making whereof I commit to cunning cooke, and teeth to eate them in the rich mans mouth.' When ordering the eglantine for your garden, be certain to specify *Rosa eglanteria* to make certain you get the true one.

These three roses are simply 'musts' for the herb garden. They are the old-fashioned species of roses that have not been hybridized and are grown for their wonderful, matchless fragrance and their food value. The petals of the damask and the Provence rose are used, both fresh and dried, for flavouring dishes and candies of all types. The eglantine contributes its primary 'hips', the fleshy swollen bases that ultimately enclose the fruit. These roses are also grown widely for use in potpourri. For this they must be planted on a much larger scale, since the number of petals needed in potpourri is far greater than the number needed for cooking.

All of these roses are so highly steeped in history and romance that no attempt will be made to cover this phase. It is hoped that what has been said here will provide the incentive for you to grow them in your herb garden and arouse within you the curiosity to find out more about their historical background by reading Shakespeare's *Henry VI*.

RUE
Ruta graveolens
of the Rutaceae
family

Among the ancient Greeks and Romans rue was highly esteemed as a seasoning for food and for use in medicine. It was especially noted for the latter, and even in Pliny's time it was considered to be beneficial for eighty-four maladies. Although rue is certainly a bitter and active plant, so are many of the other materials we use every day to make wonderful concoctions.

Rue is a handsome plant for any herb garden. It does very well as a hedge in small gardens and as a border for pathways. Once you have seen the plant in full and mature growth, it will find its way into your heart, and the next thing you know—it will be in your herb garden.

It grows to a height of two feet and this fact will be of interest to flower arrangers. They will also be attracted by its umbels of yellow flowers that cover the lacy blue-green leaves; the flowers bloom all summer long and are borne in corymbs or short terminal clusters on the plant. Rue can be grown from seed, from cuttings, from layers, or by division of the tufts. No special directions are needed except to point out that it prefers a rather poor clay soil. In fact, some people suggest that it be planted in the most barren part of the garden. There is a widespread use of rue in connection with the many ailments common to poultry.

Rue also needs sunshine most of the time. Remember that if the soil is too rich and fertile the plant will sometimes be killed by the frost, but in hardy and poor soil it seems to challenge the elements to the utmost of its being. For further growing information please refer to the 'Herb Growing Charts' in Chapter 5.

Shakespeare was well aware of the virtues of rue and mentioned it along with rosemary as a beauty aid and disinfectant. Other references can be found in *Richard II*.

SAGE
Salvia officinalis
of the Boraginaceae
family

Certainly the most colourful, historically speaking, of all the herbs, sage is probably the most widely used herb both in Britain and the United States. This statement probably applies to the entire world. It can safely be said that it is universally employed as a seasoning or flavouring.

Sage has been cultivated since the earliest days of recorded history. It stemmed originally from the northern shores of the Mediterranean. So wide has been its acceptance that there is scarcely an ancient scholar or naturalist who has not described it profusely in his writings. Theophrastus, Dioscorides, and Pliny all mentioned sage at great length. There is much legend spun in with the plant's history. No attempt has been made here even to touch upon it. After you have grown sage in your own herb garden and used the freshly picked leaves, your curiosity will provide the incentive to learn more of this phase of the story.

This hardy perennial reaches upward about two feet but it rarely blooms until the second season of growth. Its stems are covered with a soft, velvety down and from them spring the leaf stems. The leaves are most unusual in that they change from sage green to grey back to sage green, et cetera, at different seasons. They tend to be round and are darker on top than on the underside. They are covered with soft white hairs. The leaves are usually bursting, literally, with the oil that *is* sage and the fragrance of the entire plant is similar to that of a mixture of thyme, turpentine, and a pleasant pungent material with a hint of camphor trying to find its place in the crowded theatre. The plant produces flowers in June that are just about the loveliest blue spikes I have ever seen. Besides the many culinary uses for sage, it has much fragrance and beauty to offer in the garden.

When the leaves are picked, only the perfect green ones are selected; on drying they turn greyish in colour. The leaves are used to flavour pork, veal, sausages, goose and other poultry stuffings among many other things. Commercial meat-packing houses are the largest users. In the industrial field, an oil is extracted from the entire plant for use primarily in soaps and perfumes. We import more than two million pounds per year.

SANTOLINAS
of the
Compositae
family

Lavender Cotton (*Santolina chamaecyparissus*)
Emerald Green (*Sanbtolina virens*)

Just the name seems to express most of the well-known attributes of santolina. The name seems to mean something good, unusual, and even slightly exotic. There are five or more santolina variations in the mint family, and all of them have a magnificent, intriguing beauty. Since they are grown in the herb garden primarily for their ornamental effect (but not entirely—they still are used somewhat in the kitchen), the lavender cotton and the emerald green santolinas have been selected for this space. Their beauty is elegant, classical, and overflowing with fragrance.

LAVENDER COTTON is a hardy perennial with silver-grey foliage. The foliage stems are so branching that compactness seems to be built into the plant; the over-all effect remains one of a tiny grey coral. The leaves are tiny and inconspicuous, yet interwoven into the plant as a whole with a fine architectural touch. This santolina is a native of southern Europe and particularly southern France. It resembles lemon or chartreuse co-ordinated button designs. It contains a pungent essential oil, but the pungency in this one is probably the most pleasing you have ever experienced. The flowers have some medicinal use against ringworm, while the leafy stems are used mainly in perfumes and bouquets for linen closets. Lavender cotton likes a very sunny spot and it should not be pruned too often inasmuch as this tends to retard growth. It is not a really hardy plant and therefore should be protected against the winter snows.

THE EMERALD GREEN SANTOLINA is just as wondrous as the lavender cotton, but in a different way. Its foliage is so dense that it resembles an evergreen cypress. The tinsel-like foliage contains an oil with a racy fragrance made up of a pleasing combination of menthol and peppermint. The flowers resemble those of lavender cotton. The emerald green is a rapid grower and, since it finds wide usage as a hedging, it must be kept cropped and compact.

Lavender cotton grows to a height of eighteen inches, while the emerald green reaches up to twenty-four inches. Once you have seen, touched, and known the experience of santolina, your herb garden will never be without it.

For a delightful fragrance in your clothes cupboards, try this: in small cheesecloth bags or plastic boxes with holes in the lid put 2 tablespoons crushed cloves, 2 tablespoons cinnamon, $\frac{1}{4}$ cup dried and crumbled mint, tansy, lemon balm, and santolina.

SAVORY of the mint family

Summer Savory (*Satureia hortensis*)
Winter Savory (*Satureia montana*)

SUMMER
SAVORY
Satureia hortensis

Another of the true herb classics is before us, beckoning with pale, pinkish-lavender fingers that look like short spikes made of whorls in the axils of the green. They are beckoning for us to come to the land of fragrance, flavour, and beauty. The fingers are on arms that will reach a height of about eighteen inches; the entire body or complete plant of summer savory has been said to be the most satisfactory and useful of all the annual herbs.

Summer savory is one of the dainty, delicate herbs that contributes everything desirable to the herb garden—fragrance and beauty outside, fragrance and flavour in the kitchen. It is native to southern Europe and is used in that section of the world by all chefs as a culinary vegetable that puts a delightful, appetizing aroma into their food dishes. Summer savory is used with loving tenderness by all cooks who know anything at all about herbs, for the reason that was recently given by an expert in the field of cooking with herbs and spices. He said that every cook should remember at all times that the function of an herb is to bring out, and not black out, the flavour of a food. Summer savory brings out the flavour in many different types of foods, either singly or in combination. There are more than one hundred recipes available for its use and these cover a world of different bouquets.

Summer savory is a favourite with all 'pleasure gardeners', who like to show its beautiful blossoms in edging for borders. They are particularly fond of its piquant, sweet fragrance. The tender leaves may be used any time during the season, and in some seasons it is possible

G   97

to cut several crops. When used fresh, the leaves should not have been cut for any appreciable length of time. The leaves can be dried for winter use by tying small bunches together and keeping them in a proper storage place during the drying. When the leaves are thoroughly dry they should be stripped from the stems and stored in tightly covered jars. These can be of great help in making *fines herbes* mixtures.

WINTER SAVORY
Satureia montana

This is the more hardy member of the savories. The perennial evergreen is a native of the Mediterranean region and normally grows to a height of about one foot but across the top it will generally measure up to two feet. With its touch-of-pink white flowers and its rich green leaves, winter savory adds a real touch of beauty to the herb garden. It has all the virtues of summer savory except that it is slightly more pungent.

SESAME
Sesamum orientale
of the Pedaliaceae
family

'Open sesame!' is a phrase familiar to practically every civilized person in the world and immediately brings to mind the tales of the Arabian Nights. Far older than the tales of the Arabian Nights is the plant itself. Sesame has been grown for uncounted centuries, especially in the Far East, where it is still used on a large scale. Sesame is often referred to as benne, and this apparently comes from benne (or Benny) oil, which is made from sesame seeds and is used almost exclusively in Africa and the Orient for cooking and in medicines.

To the herb gardener of the West, the oil for cooking would be of no interest since other cooking oils are plentiful and inexpensive. The plant itself, however, is a beauteous thing in the garden. The stems are round, rather heavy but glistening, and grow to a height of three feet (they have been known to shoot up to a height of five or six feet). On the stems will be found leaves of a different nature and size from top to bottom. At the lower end the leaves are opposite and rather fleshy, while the upper leaves are not toothed but are rather slender and placed along the stem alternately. The blooming season for sesame is one of the longest of all the herbs and continues from July to September in most sections of the country. The flowers are the essence of beauty: lavender-tinted whites, resembling foxglove.

The historical background of sesame is intriguing. According to some, sesame was created by Yama, God of Death, who, after a long penitence, gave his blessing to its various uses, which included funerals and expiatory ceremonies in which it was used as a purifier and symbol of immortality. Both Theophrastus and Dioscorides mentioned sesame in various writings.

Sesame was introduced into the United States by the African Negroes who were brought here. They first cultivated it in Florida. From there it has spread throughout the rest of the United States and Canada. One of the highest compliments ever paid to this herb was that of Ibn of Baithar, who is reported to have said that sesame oil 'from the seed' is a good cure for dandruff when used with other oils such as olive oil and myrtle oil!

Sesame is one of the few herbs that has a very definite place in the field of medicine; it is listed in all pharmacopoeias. The oil from the seeds can be used as a soothing external rubbing medium or can be used internally as a mild laxative. In the south of France the oil is extracted from the seed for use in the manufacture of soap.

The primary cooking oil in China, Egypt, and India is that extracted from sesame seed; it is used like olive oil in cooking. Many of our local natives make a hearty meal constructed around sesame seeds that are parched over a fire, then mixed with water, and finally stewed with other ingredients. In some parts of the South there are

natives who make broths from the seeds and at times they candy them
with sugar or molasses.

The herb gardener will be interested in the sesame plant primarily
from three points of view, and these are: beauty and fragrance in the
garden; stalks for exotic flower arrangements; the widespread use of
sesame seeds on the outside of buns, rolls, and cookies. When the
seeds are slightly crunched, a very pleasing fragrance and flavour are
emitted.

The sesame plant is easy to grow. It is an annual and, though it
is classified as a tropical annual, it can be grown like an ordinary
annual.

SHALLOT
Allium
ascalonicum
of the lily family

The lily family seems to cover a wider range of flavours than any
other family, with the onion, garlic, chives, leek, rocambole, and now
shallot, one of the very mild members of the family. It is classified as
an onion-like herb that is grown the same way onions are. Besides
being much milder than the onion, shallot has one major physical
difference. Instead of growing one large bulb, with offsets, the mature
bulb of shallot looks very much like that of garlic: a series of sections
(cloves) that will come apart rather easily.

It is sometimes called eschallot. Shallot is a native of western Asia
and was named for a town called Ascalon in Palestine. When allowed
to flower in cultivation, small head clusters of flowers appear, sometimes white and sometimes violet. Just as in the case of leek, the shallot
can be used in almost any culinary delight if the flavour of the onion
and other members of the lily family seem to be too flavourful to 'fit'.

The foliage resembles that of the onion. The young mild leaves are frequently harvested for greens as bunch onions.

Which member of the lily family you prefer depends upon what you are eating, the strength of flavour desired, and the condition of your palate. In many cases, shallot is just right. Try it sometime with ordinary brown beans or white navy beans. It's a different taste, milder and, to some, more satisfying.

SORREL

> French Sorrel (*Rumex scutatus*)
> Garden Sorrel (*Rumex acetosa*)
> Wood Sorrel (*Oxalis violacea*)
> of the Polygonaceae family

FRENCH
SORREL
Rumex scutatus

Three sorrels should be covered here, since each is a very definite part of the 'big herb picture'. The first is the French sorrel (*Rumex scutatus*), which has always been very dear to the hearts of all French people. The French have known of sorrel and its many wonders almost since the beginning of their recorded history. Their love for the plant is connected particularly with its bright green beauty in the herb garden and its very long succulent leaves in salads, one of their favourite dishes. There is scarcely a particle of the sorrel plant that the French do not utilize. It is cooked just as we cook spinach. The French sorrel is of the low-growing variety and has beautiful bitter-sweet, lush, crisp green leaves. Another great feature to the French is the fact that sorrel takes only sixty days to grow and be ready for cutting and using. It is also a very hardy perennial and the plants will continue to produce leaves for their fine beauty and exquisite flavour for up to five years. After this time some horticulturists suggest that the plants be re-sown.

The French sorrel has an almost unbelievable lemon-like tang that can be enjoyed in many dishes such as consommé, soups, fish, omelettes, and scrambled eggs. It has also been found to be excellent with lamb, beef, and many vegetables.

GARDEN
SORREL
Rumex acetosa

The second sorrel is the garden sorrel (*Rumex acetosa*), which grows to a much larger over-all size than French sorrel. It has oblong leaves and arrow-shaped bases. This particular sorrel will grow to a height of three feet. In early spring it is almost tasteless but as the season progresses the acid taste in the plant becomes more pronounced.

Garden sorrel thrives particularly well in moist soil. The plants should be dug up, divided, and replanted every four or five years. The garden sorrel is as delectable to some as the French sorrel; it is particularly savoury in soups and salads. There is one feature about garden sorrel that really sets it apart from all of the other herbs: it is used in diets designed to overcome a deficiency of vitamin C in the body.

WOOD
SORREL
Oxalis acetosella
of the Oxalidaceae
family

The third sorrel is the little wood sorrel (*Oxalis*), which is a native of Europe. It came to America with the earliest settlers. Since its arrival in America it has been found growing all the way from Nova Scotia to North Carolina. The little wood sorrel below the base is made up of tiny bulblets and prefers moist, shady places to find complete contentment. It has been called sourgrass by people who have made it a practice to transplant these tiny bulblets to their herb garden.

One of the most outstanding attractions of wood sorrel is the great contribution it makes to any shady border with its clover-shaped leaves and dainty flowers, which are often pink, lavender, or yellow. Darwin has described at great length the power and movement in plants and in particular the wood sorrel plant. This is what he has to say about wood sorrel: 'This little plant goes to sleep at night—it trembles and folds into its shy little self at the least change of temperature.'

Wood sorrel is acclaimed for other famous characteristics, among which is the fact that it is called the true shamrock of ancient Ireland; it is also claimed to be the alleluia plant because it blooms at Eastertime. The herb gardener who puts wood sorrel in his garden will certainly find the greatest pleasure in using the tiny cloverlike leaves as a garnish for fruit salads. In colonial times the children used to nibble the leaves as they gathered them for use in early spring puddings.

These are the three sorrels and each has its own set of attractions. One or more of the sorrels should be in every herb garden.

SWEET BASIL
Ocimum basilicum
of the mint family

Sweet Basil is one of the most popular seasoning herbs known to the world today, and one of the reasons for this is the fact that it has within it the ability to make savoury the most inexpensive food dishes. It will be recalled that in olden days one of the primary reasons for using spices and herbs was either to make unpalatable food taste better or inexpensive food taste delightful. The basils, of which from fifty to sixty species are grown in the warmer parts of the world, are extremely fragrant and flavourful to the palate.

An old saying goes: 'Good things come in small packages', and this certainly must be true of the basils, particularly sweet basil. It is a bushy plant that grows in some warmer climates to a height of eighteen inches. It is not a many-stemmed plant, but the leaves are particularly unusual in that each pair of opposite leaves is covered with a bloom, yet they glisten on both sides with specks of oil from the reservoirs present. The undersurface is slightly downy. The greatest feature of these unusual leaves, however, is the licorice-and-spice taste when fresh, and when dried a fragrance suggesting a combination of lemon, anise, resin, and spice. No other herb seems to possess this complete versatility of bouquet patterns from the fresh to the dry stage.

The flowers of sweet basil are very beautiful and come at the end of July and August. Although they are small, in pairs and almost inconspicuous, their greenish whiteness seems to add a flair to the plant that is not found in other herbal plants.

Sweet basil is another of the most widely used seasoning herbs and it is often combined with other herbs in mixtures for various preparations. By itself it seems to give its best performance in imparting an almost matchless taste to dishes made with tomatoes, cheese, and eggs. It is also a fine addition to vinegars, various types of soups, many vegetables, most of the meats, some butter sauces, and any other dish in which you can imagine the faint yet distinct bouquet of something resembling 'pepperish clove'.

One unusual use for sweet basil is as a kind of snuff. Apparently there are still some quaint old ladies who use the powdered leaves for this purpose.

Although sweet basil is being utilized on a large scale, much experimentation remains to be done. A little time spent in the kitchen trying it in new ways should bring exciting taste experiences.

There is another prominent type of basil called bush basil, which is also a neat, bushy, small plant. It is more compact and branched than sweet basil. The outstanding feature of bush basil is that it is extremely fragrant of lemon and spice and its flavour can only be described as being slightly bitter, resinous but stimulating. It is suggested that you familiarize yourself completely with sweet basil before attempting to use bush basil in the kitchen.

SWEET
CICELY
Myrrhis odorata
of the parsley
family

The people from a town high in the mountains of Savoy are responsible for our having received in ancient times one of the most esteemed plants known to mankind. Sweet cicely is this plant and it goes back far in history, even to biblical times. Gerard and Pliny mentioned it, as did Parkinson, who said, 'It gives a better taste to any other herb put with it'. Seeds were crushed in olden days for their pleasantly fragrant oil, which was used to scent and polish floors and furniture made from oak.

The plant grows two to three feet high and it has very narrow stems. The leaves are much divided, and it is this quality that builds into the foliage architecture the plant's fernlike effect. The polygamous flowers are small and white, reminding one of well-drilled soldiers in the umbel that holds them. The seeds are the most aromatic part of the plant.

As to modern-day uses of sweet cicely, the seeds are used widely in flavouring beverages, especially chartreuse, one of the finest cordials in the world, which is made by Carthusian monks. Sweet cicely is also used to flavour foods, primarily in France. The seeds represent the largest potential use of the plant. They have one remarkable quality that sets them apart from other herbs: the ability to act as a synergist when blending with anything, so long as there is another herb in it. As a synergist, sweet cicely makes the flavour of the final blend so much more palate-pleasing than any of the ingredients tasted alone.

SWEET
WOODRUFF
Asperula odorata
of the madder
family

This sweet-smelling, low-growing plant comes to us from Europe and the Orient. It is a naturalized citizen now and loved by all who have had the pleasure of making its acquaintance. This herb is aptly described by Gerard: 'The Woodrooffe hath many square stalks full of joints, and every knot or joynt seven or eight long narrow leaves, set round about like a star, or the rowell of a spurr, the flowers grow at the top of the stems, of a white color and of a very sweet smell, which being made up into garlands, or bundles, and hanging up in the heat of summer, doth very well attemper the aire, coole and make fresh the place, to the delight and comfort of such as are therein.'

The fragrance of sweet woodruff, the scent of new-mown hay, has made this low-growing herb a favourite for ground covers in the shady and moist places in the pleasure garden. It can also be used as the grace notes in a flower arrangement. The deep green starlike whorls of leaves and the small white star flowers would be especially interesting to children arranging flowers. It flowers in June and July.

It is ornamental and fragrant and has much to give in flavour (fascinating in fruit cups). Refreshing bouquet is yours with sweet woodruff in beverages, and it puts exquisite aroma into sachets.

There is another woodruff that should be mentioned here. Its botanical name is *Asperula oriental azurea*. A splendid airy effect is obtained with its azure-blue flowers, which tend to relieve the heaviness of the more abundant flowers in the herb garden.

TANSY
Tanacetum vulgare
of the Compositae
family

The definition of a flower garden should, in addition to describing the garden, include a list of flowers to guide the uninitiated in planning a garden. Tansy should be on this list. Then any book on flower arrangements should include tansy on the list of plants most used by arrangers who need a fernlike background.

The roots are perennial and they easily develop themselves again at the first signs of spring. From the roots grow a great number of stems, up to three feet above the ground, erect, sturdy, and covered with fernlike leaves. The leaves are much divided, with oval, oblong outlines, rich green, slightly downy on the underside and smooth above. These bear an abundance of small yellow flower heads in unusually crowded corymbs. Greyish-looking seeds follow the flowers. A caution should be added here: tansy is a robust weedy plant that soon grows into thick clumps.

According to folklore, it must be taken internally in the spring to avoid the summer sickness. We are also told that it has been rubbed over raw meat to keep flies away and prevent decay. 'Winter posies' are supposedly kept fresh-looking and smiling by the flowers that retain their yellow colour all winter. Tansy has been grown in our country so long that it appeared in Prince's great catalogue, printed in 1790, and in the one published by Bartram in 1814.

Although tansy was put through most of the same medicinal trials as other well-known herbs, the *National Standard Dispensary* says today that it has no medicinal value and is really quite poisonous when taken internally. Modern medical herbalists do not agree with this and use small doses of the fluid extract in female complaints. Some people also use it sparingly in medicines for application to the human body and to animals. This and the use of small quantities of tansy oil, distilled from the tops and leaves, in toilet waters from time to time, represent tansy outside of the ornamental garden. It has been used in teas and puddings.

The plant is a native of southern Europe and, unlike most herbs, it likes heavy soils. However, it does well in any good garden soil. Remember, too, that tansy likes plenty of sun. In the United States, Michigan produces far more tansy than any other state.

Tansy stands for truly sense-pleasing fragrance and beauty and it should be in your garden.

TARRAGON
Artemisia
dracunculus
of the Compositae
Artemisia family

Tarragon is a fairly hardy perennial that is supposed to be a native of southern Russia, Siberia, and Tartary. It is estimated that tarragon has been cultivated for about five hundred years, and this relatively new herb is becoming more and more prominent in America. There are two reasons for its popularity: tarragon leaves are widely used with steaks, chops, in salads, fish sauce, preserves, pickles, mustard, mayonnaise, and of course in tarragon vinegar; tarragon leafy tops go into the commercial markets to flavour confectionery and to make perfumes and toilet waters.

It is one of the few herbs that is known not to set seed, which means, of course, that propagation is by cuttings or root division. It is a graceful plant when full grown, and the leaves seem to have a fragrance and flavour about them similar to that of anise. The plant has a great number of branching stems on which are found lance-shaped leaves and white flowers that are sterile.

In tarragon you have another wonderful specimen for your herb garden. It has the beauty and the fragrance required outside and it most certainly has the fragrance and flavour required inside. This is another herb that will be of interest to the flower arranger because of its convenient height range.

THYME
Thymus vulgaris
of the mint family

This famous, beautiful, versatile herb could well be referred to as 'Old Father Thyme' since it seems to have been with us almost as long as the real Father Time. Since very early days, it has been cultivated for culinary uses, but, like all of the better-known herbs, it was once grown and used on a large scale for its supposed medicinal value. It is cultivated now almost entirely for cookery and, next to sage, is probably the most widely used herb.

The name is from the Greek word *thymon*, or sacrifice; it was used as an incense to perfume the temples. The Romans used thyme both in cookery and as a bee forage. If you have garden space for only a few herbs, be sure to include thyme. It is an ideal ornament for use as a dwarf facer or a border planting. It generally grows to a height of about eight inches, with slender wood stems and oblong tapering leaves that are deep green on top and grey underneath. The flowers, which generally appear in June, form whorls and leafy spikes of lavender-pink in the upper leaves.

Thyme is a native of dry, stony places along the coasts of the Mediterranean but has been naturalized in most civilized countries, regardless of climate. It seems to thrive best in rather poor but limey soil; at least it can be said that some of the wonderful fragrance is missing when it is grown in heavy soils. Seeds should be planted in April or May in a special seed bed that can be kept partially shaded and moist (even though the plant likes full sun when once started). Transplanting can be done when the plants are well out of the soil; they may be set in the field during June or even as late as July, preferably just before or just after a shower. Although thyme is a perennial, it becomes less aromatic after the first two years of growth, so it is suggested that a new sowing be made every second year.

All parts of the thyme plant are fragrant because of its wonderful aromatic, volatile oil, which makes up about one per cent of the total plant. The oil is extracted on a commercial scale, primarily in France, and it is used extensively in perfumery. The fresh tops are used as a garnish, the leaves, either fresh or dried, are chopped and used in flavouring a wide variety of cooked foods. There is scarcely a cook who does not use it almost every day. The dried form of thyme as obtained in the markets does an excellent job of putting zest into our foods, with its very pleasant, bitter tang. The many uses of thyme are listed in the Herb Chart in Chapter 4.

There is a related plant, lemon thyme, with lemon-scented foliage. It is carried by dealers under the name *Thymus serpyllum canadense.*

WINTER-
GREEN
Gaultheria
procumbens
of the Ericaceae or
heath family

Once this tiny and bountiful wonder of nature has been seen in the shady woodland, peeping proudly from its leafy perch, one cannot resist the impulse to provide space for it in the herb garden—or at least in the wild flower area of the herb garden. It is somewhat particular about its home site, as it cannot be enjoyed everywhere. But if it can be given a home site based on an acid-type soil with a litter of pine needles or oak leaves, and a bit of sunlight filtered through open woods, you will find it to be a happy little plant and it will share its happiness with you.

The wintergreen is a perennial and a native of America. This hardy little plant has always been a joy to children fortunate enough to have had the opportunity to go mountain 'tea' picking, or searching for the tender, spicy leaves of the wintergreen. When a patch was found, they would chew some of the young yellowish-green leaves tinted with red on the spot and gather some to take home for tea making. The location was always marked so that they could be certain of finding their way back in October for teaberry picking. The delicious red 'teaberry', which has a mealy taste on the tongue, is loved by woods creatures as much as by the children. Bobwhites, quail, pheasant, and deer nibble on the berries and leaves to acquire a little spiciness in their diet.

Wintergreen usually will grow from two to six inches in height and the plants seem to like to gather together in groups. The stems push upward from the underground scaly bark stems. They are smooth below and downy and crowned with leaves above. The leaves, which are quite large for the size of the plant, are oval and, when young, are a combination of yellow, green, and red. The older leaves are green above and yellow-green below. When the young leaves are crushed between the fingers, they smell as though you had peppermint candy in your hand. The flowers are small, and bloom from June to September. Brilliant red berries come in October. They are delicious when eaten in the coolness of the woods.

Early Americans used the leaves of wintergreen to make tea during the Revolution and many Americans enjoy this tea today. For more than two hundred years the wintergreen plant was our only source of oil of wintergreen, which is still the best external application for the aches and pains of rheumatism. Though now it can be produced chemically more cheaply, it is questionable whether the synthetic oil is as effective as that extracted from the plant.

Its beauty and uniqueness make it more than eligible for your garden. I have transplanted the creeping wintergreen to the wild flower area in my herb garden and there it is growing happily beside the wild ginger and the May apples.

YARROW
*Achillea
millefolium*
of the Compositae
family

Here is one of the very oldest known herbs or, rather, weeds, as it is known today. Actually all over the world it is called the commonest of common weeds. It is so prevalent everywhere that one wonders at the marvellous scheme it employs to overrun the earth. It has been given broad coverage in the mythology, folklore, medicine, and literature of many peoples. Achilles learned of the virtues of yarrow from Chiron, the Centaur, in order that he might make an ointment that would heal his Myrmidons (Thessalian warriors) who were wounded in the siege of Troy. Divers properties have been attributed to it: it has been used as a love charm and as an herb tea brewed by old crones to cure anything from loss of hair to the ague. It has also been mentioned as an ingredient of an especially intoxicating beer made by the Swedes. Another use was based on yarrow's supposed ability to induce nosebleed for relief of congestive headache.

Yarrow is a pleasant-looking plant, despite its classification as the 'commonest of all common weeds'. Actually it has the lacy-looking structure and form of Gothic architecture and detail. Flower arrangers who have not worked with it will be pleasantly surprised at the charm, beauty, and unusualness it will add to any church arrangement. A very leafy plant, it has erect stems that usually grow to a height of one to two feet. The leaves are really a very pretty shade of green. Its flowering season is from June to November, one of the longest of any of the plants. The flowers are pink or greyish-white, depending somewhat upon growing conditions.

Although yarrow now finds practically no way into the culinary field, it is definitely a part of the 'Big Herb Picture' and the herb gardener should have some knowledge of it, if only for history's sake. With its lacelike foliage pattern, yarrow gives the appearance of being made up of feathery masses. And there is nothing more pleasing in a quiet, hushed way than to catch a breath of the wholesome, autumnal, nutty odour of its flowers.

As a medicinal means of inducing perspiration in the treatment of colds and influenza, it is one of the most widely used diaphoretics and febrifuges in modern herbal therapy. Some claim that the regular periodic use of yarrow is a safeguard against colds, maintaining a cleansing function of the pores of the skin.

4. Herb chart: culinary and household uses of herbs

AMBROSIA   Romantic and fragrant ambrosia has been used by the ancients for flavouring and fragrance since recorded history. Use for fruit cups, beverages, salads, preserves, jellies, and potpourri.

ANGELICA   This herb with its lovely-sounding name has many uses, from candies to cordials to a boiled salad. The muscatel flavour is good in custards and desserts.

ANISE   Seeds used for liqueurs, cordials, fruit salads, vegetable salads, coffeecake, baked apples, rolls, shellfish, sea-food salads.

BALM   Fresh leaves used for pleasing, stimulating teas and beverages. Fragrant and dainty in finger bowls.

BERGAMOT   Fresh leaves used in fruit cups, punch, teas, beverages, for fragrant potpourri, and for colour in the herb garden. Nice in flower arrangements.

BETONY   Refreshing teas and beverages; a conversation piece in the herb or wild flower garden.

BORAGE   Prettiest of all herbs, with lovely grey leaves and sky-blue flowers. Select the tender green leaves to use with fish, potatoes, cottage cheese, new peas. Use flowers to garnish punch, fruit salads, and beverages.

BURNET

Fresh leaves used for teas and beverages, cooked salads, green salads, in cottage cheese, and for garnishes.

CALAMUS

Use to flavour creams, puddings, and custards, also for colour and fragrance in the garden.

CAMOMILE

Use for teas and beverages made to keep the grower well and beautiful, as it is said to be good for indigestion and complexion! To make the hair soft after shampoos, one should always rinse the hair with a solution of camomile. The ancients say, Grow camomile about the herb garden to keep all other plants happy.

CARAWAY

Use for French dressing, cottage cheese, herb breads, cakes, and salads.

CATNIP

Fresh leaves used for teas and garnishes as you would use mint leaves. A little 'nip' of the fresh leaves is especially pleasing to your cats and kittens.

CHERVIL

Said to be the most delicately flavoured of all the herbs. Use the leaves fresh or dried. Perfect in cheese dishes, butter sauces with baked chicken and green salads.

CHICORY

Roots are used, cooked with butter, as a green vegetable. Roasted, roots can be added to coffee or used as a coffee substitute. The stalks, blanched, may be used like celery.

CHIVES

Use for salads and salad dressing, liver, creamed beef, cottage cheese, cream cheese, hot buttered popcorn, new potatoes, baby green peas, corn, scrambled eggs, devilled eggs, broiled tomatoes.

CLARY

Sometimes called muscatel sage. Try with baked chicken, omelettes, beverages, and teas. Use flowers and leaves for garnishes.

CORIANDER — Seeds are used in broth, or mashed and used for poultry, pickles, bread, and cookies.

COSTMARY — Has a lovely mild flavour—nice with veal or chicken. Fresh or dried leaves make a very pleasant tea.

CRESSES — Upland: cooked green salads, tossed green salads.
Water: sandwiches, garnishes, and salads. Especially good with sardines and cream cheese.
Garden: cooked like spinach, mixed with greens for salads.

CUMIN — Use seed or fruit when you want a highly seasoned stimulating flavour for sauces, gravies, spaghetti, chili dishes, devilled eggs, pork or tamale pie. Perfect for pizza pies.

DANDELION — Use young leaves for cooked green salad or fresh salad; use blossoms for wine.

DILL — Use for cucumber pickles, fish, chopped steak, potatoes, roast duck, potato salad.

FENNEL and FENNEL FLOWER — Use for salads, soups, sauces, apple pie, garnishes. The stems and bulbs are served raw like celery.

FEVERFEW — Good for medicinal teas, wonderful as a background plant, and lovely in flower arrangements.

GARLIC — Always use cutting boards so other foods do not pick up flavours. Good for baked beans, ripe olives, vegetables, salads, sauces, French dressing, Swiss steak, hamburgers, spaghetti, potato salad, cheese spreads, French bread, lamb roasts, and cooked spinach.

GERANIUM	Beautiful fragrant leaves are used in custards, puddings, jellies, and desserts, as garnish for jellied salads and desserts. Nice for table arrangements.
GERMANDER	Mostly used for ornamental border planting in the herb garden. Mint-flavoured leaves used for fragrance, sometimes for flavour.
HOP	The flower buds are cooked for salads. Tea made from buds. Liquid put into breads to make them lighter.
HOREHOUND	Grow for candies and old-fashioned teas.
HORSE-RADISH	Use for beef dishes, oysters, shrimp, crab cakes, sauces, and dips.
HYSSOP	Use in beverages, soups and salads.
LAVENDER	Grown mostly for fragrance and beauty in the garden, it has been used for flavouring. At your next garden club luncheon, use the flowers to garnish your fruit cups.
LEEK	Use in salads, soups, and stews or for fresh tidbit trays.
LEMON VERBENA	Use for fragrant, fresh-looking finger bowls. For beverages and teas, use to garnish fruit salads and for a conversation piece. Place leaves on a crystal plate, set honeydew wedge on leaves, top with a paper-thin slice of pink ham.
LOVAGE	Seeds are used to flavour desserts and confections. The stems can be candied. The stalks can be blanched and eaten like celery.
POT MARIGOLD	Buds can be cooked in oil and used in salads and as food colouring. Best as a colour interest in the herb garden.

MARJORAMS — Can be used fresh or dried. Use for eggs, stuffings, poultry, cheese, meat stews, lamb, beef, pork, veal, baked fish, Swiss steak, cream sauces, gravies, soups, vegetables: lima beans, string beans, and even spinach!

MAY APPLE — Decorative in the garden. Apples can be eaten when ripe for an unusual flavour.

MINTS — Apple: leaves used fresh for beverages, teas, and garnishes, also decorative in the herb garden. Lovely in flower arrangements in pewter containers.

Peppermint: dried fresh or extract is used for jellies, sauces, fruit cups, fresh drinks, salads, confections, meat, begetables, and vinegars. Peppermint is delightful added to new green peas.

Spearmint: use the cool refreshing fragrant leaves to garnish veverages and teas. Crush leaves to extract oils for sherbets and ices. Use for mint sauces, coleslaw, fruit cups, salads, mint jellies, and flower arrangements. Especially lovely dried for winter bouquets.

MUSTARDS — Leaves for cooked salad greens, seeds for seasonings and flavouring. Prepared mustard sauce.

NASTURTIUM — Flowers for luncheon table arrangements. Leaves for salads and garnishes, pods or seeds for pickles and sauces.

ORÉGANO — Use either dried or fresh for soups, sauces, omelettes, crown roast pork, potatoes, pizza, veal, chili con carne, beef, rabbit, lamb, chicken, pheasant, sea food, frankfurters, stuffings, salads, all tomato dishes, stews, cabbage, broccoli.

PARSLEY

Use either fresh or dried for garnishes, cheese, eggs, meat, fish, poultry, salads, sauces, vegetables, such as new potatoes, soups.

PENNYROYAL

Use as you would mints for teas, beverages, and garnishes, also for fragrance in potpourri.

PEPPERS

Tabasco: use for pizza pies, sausage, soups, and stews.
Chili: Mexican dishes, spaghetti, beans, and cauliflower.
Ornamental and colourful in the herb garden.

POPPY

Seeds used to flavour breads, cakes, pie crust, vegetables, German and English boiled dinners. Try decorating open-face cheese sandwiches or hors d'oeuvres.

RHUBARB

Lovely for punches, pies, sauces and combines nicely with fresh strawberries. Wonderful for large flower arrangements.

ROCAMBOLE

Use like garlic. Has a much milder flavour.

ROSEMARY

Use either fresh or dried for fruit cups, fruit salads, sauces, stews, soups, veal, pork, lamb, chicken, fish, duck, beans, cauliflower.

ROSES

Damask: for lovely fragrance in sachets, potpourri, and flavourings.
Provence: candied rose petals, cakes, and jellies.
Eglantine: seed pods eaten as tasty little apples.

RUE

Use for stimulating sandwiches and tasty salads.

SAGE

Use either dry or fresh in sausage, roast pork, turkey dressing, chicken, sardine sandwiches, chicken dumplings, scalloped bananas, biscuits or meat pie topping, cottage cheese, tomatoes, baked beans.

SANTOLINAS

For ornamental beauty and lovely fragrance use for sachets, potpourri, or clothes closets. Try a fresh bouquet in your tub for a refreshing fragrance!

SAVORY

Use either dry or fresh in green salad, eggs, stuffings, or vegetables. Especially delightful piquant flavour for tossed salads. Use to season when cooking with dry wines. Winter savory is available all winter and is one of the most used of all the herbs. Use for soups, salads, stews, fried chicken, pork chops, veal, and beef.

SESAME

The small oval seeds have a fine crisp taste. Good when used in cookies, candies, cakes, and rolls. Wonderful when used in pastry for fruit pies.

SHALLOT

The green blades are sometimes used in a cooked green salad. Has a mild onion flavour.

SORREL

Cook like spinach, or use tender green leaves for salads. Little wood sorrel is a dainty garnish.

SWEET BASIL

Use for tomatoes, green peas, spaghetti sauce, vegetable juice cocktail, stews, soups, eggplant, cheese, fish sauce, shrimp and lobster. Fresh basil can be added to new potatoes, green peas, sauces.

SWEET CICELY

The seeds can be eaten fresh and green. This little herb is said to give all other herbs a better flavour when combined with others. Especially good in beverages and cordials, fruit salads and fruit cups. Leaves can be used when you want a mild anise flavour.

SWEET WOODRUFF

Use for May Day drinks and teas. Lovely for sachets and potpourri.

TANSY

Mostly used for ornamental effect and cutting greens for flower arrangements. Also used for puddings and cakes.

TARRAGON

Use either dry or fresh for sweetbreads, chicken, meat, fish, sauces, salad dressings (French and Russian), eggs, poultry, game, pickles, preserves, roast beef, cabbage, sauerkraut, slaw, stews, soups, mushrooms, lobster (broiled or stuffed).

THYME

Use either dry or fresh for stuffings, soups, chowders, meat loaves, creamed chipped beef, pork, veal, chicken, turkey, fish, potatoes, onions, eggplant, beets.

WILD GINGER

A beautiful plant in the herb garden. The leaves are used for garnishes. The aromatic roots were used by the Indians to add spiciness to Indian corn puddings, grits and hominy.

WINTERGREEN

Use fresh new leaves for tea. Lovely little red teaberries may be used for garnishes and decorations.

YARROW

Teas were made from the fresh yarrow leaves by the ancients to cure all ills, from headaches to falling hair. Today, it is a must in the herb garden for the flower arranger because of its colour range from off-white to pastel pinks.

Herb chart: culinary and household uses

CHIEF HERBS USED IN COOKERY
ARRANGED IN ORDER OF THEIR APPROXIMATE IMPORTANCE

Sage	Mint	Winter Savory
Thyme	Chervil	Cumin
Parsley	Rosemary	Fennel
Basil	Tarragon	Coriander
Summer Savory	Pot Marjoram	Anise
Sweet Marjoram	Caraway	Dill
Chives		

OUTSTANDING ROBUST HERBS FOR COOKERY

Sage	Summer Savory	Sweet Marjoram
Dill	Winter Savory	Pot Marjoram
Caraway	Horse-radish	Coriander
Fennel	Mint	Anise

MOST COMMONLY USED COMBINATIONS
OF FINES HERBES

Thyme, chervil, and basil   Chives, basil, and parsley
Chervil, parsley, and chives   Parsley, rosemary, and tarragon

Recipes*

ANGELICA CANDY

4 cups angelica stalks cut
  about 2 inches long
4 cups water

1 tablespoon salt
2 cups sugar

Soak stalks overnight in 2 cups cold water and 1 tablespoon salt. Drain off salt water and add stalks to a thick syrup made with 2 cups sugar and 2 cups water. Let stand overnight. Drain off syrup and boil to a thick consistency, add stalks, and let stand overnight. Drain candied stalks and serve. Syrup can be used for cool drinks, or rhubarb can be cooked in the syrup.

ICEBERG SALAD

1 head lettuce
¼ cup red wine vinegar
¼ cup olive oil

¼ teaspoon salt
⅛ teaspoon white pepper
¼ cup chopped chives

Tear lettuce in chunks. Put vinegar in jar, add olive oil, and shake well. Put lettuce in salad bowl, pour the wine dressing over it, and toss lightly until lettuce is well coated. Add chopped chives, salt, and pepper and toss lightly. Serve in individual wooden salad bowls. Serves 4 to 6.

CUMIN SAUCE FOR ENCHILADAS . . . PRIMARILY

1 onion, chopped
2 cloves garlic, chopped fine
2 pounds lean ground beef
3 tablespoons olive oil
¼ teaspoon salt
¼ teaspoon cayenne pepper

¼ teaspoon black pepper
2 tablespoons chili powder
½ teaspoon cumin seed
2 cups beef stock
1 can baked beans
½ can tomato paste

* See p. 152 for Beverages Recipes.

123

In a large iron skillet sauté the onion, garlic, and meat in the olive oil. Add salt, pepper, chili powder, and cumin seed. Simmer 15 minutes, stir often. Pour in stock, beans, and tomato paste and stir. Simmer on low heat for 1 hour, stirring often. Serves 4.

DILL SAUCE DE LUXE

1 *cup mayonnaise*
2 *tablespoons vinegar*
¼ *teaspoon salt*
1 *tablespoon minced sweet pickles*
½ *teaspoon Worcestershire sauce*
4 *drops Tabasco sauce*
½ *teaspoon tarragon*
1 *teaspoon parsley*
¼ *teaspoon powdered mustard*
1 *tablespoon chopped fresh dill*

Mix all ingredients thoroughly and serve from your prettiest sauce bowl with french fried shrimp or broiled fish.

DILL POTATO AND EGG SALAD

2 *hard-boiled eggs*   1 *teaspoon sugar*
3 *medium potatoes*   ¼ *teaspoon pepper*
1 *medium dill pickle*   1 *teaspoon chopped fresh dill*
1 *medium onion*   ½ *cup mayonnaise*
½ *cup mild white vinegar*   ⅛ *teaspoon paprika*
½ *teaspoon salt*

Cook potatoes until tender. Cool. Cube potatoes. Chop eggs, pickle, and onion, zdd to cubed potatoes. Add vinegar, salt, sugar, pepper, and dill to mayonnaise. Blend well, pour over potatoes. Put into your favourite salad bowl. Sprinkle paprika over salad. Chill Serves 4.

OLD-FASHIONED APPLE PIE

6 *tart apples*
1 *cup sugar*
2 *tablespoons flour*
½ *teaspoon chopped fresh sweet fennel*
2 *tablespoons butter*

Peel apples and slice very thin. Combine sugar (brown sugar may be substituted for white sugar with wonderful results), flour, and fennel. Mix with the apples. Fill 9-inch pastry-lined pie pan. Dot with butter. Bake at 450° F. about 40 minutes. Serves 6.

GARLIC CLAM CRISPS DE BLANCHE

> 1 *tablespoon butter*
> 2 *tablespoons finely chopped onion*
> 1½ *tablespoons flour*
> ½ *teaspoon Worcestershire sauce*
> ¼ *teaspoon minced garlic or*
>   *dash garlic salt*
> 1 *7½-ounce can minced clams*
> 12 *slices bread*

Melt butter in small frying pan over low heat. Sauté onion 2 or 3 minutes, add flour, and blend. Stir in Worcestershire sauce and blend. Stir in garlic and clam juice. Cook until thick. Cool. Cut crusts from thin sandwich bread. Roll each slice flat with rolling pin and spread with garlic clam mixture. Roll like a jelly roll, cut in slices. Put on well-buttered rice paper or greaseproof paper. Brush with melted butter and bake at 450° F. until brown. Serve hot with cocktails. These may be frozen and baked as needed.

CHARCOAL-BROILED STEAK À LA ED AND BETTY

> 1 *clove garlic*
> 1 *tablespoon salad oil*
> 2 *pounds flank steak*
> ¼ *teaspoon pepper*
> 1 *teaspoon salt*

Prepare charcoal burner for cooking. Cut garlic clove in half and soak in salad oil. Using ½ clove garlic for each side of steak, rub steak with garlic. Sprinkle with pepper. Place steak on broiler for 5 minutes on one side, turn, pepper, and broil 5 minutes on this side. Carve crosswise in very thin slices. Salt to taste. *Do not salt before cooking,* or you will loose valuable juices. Five minutes' cooking time on each side is for medium-rare steak. Cook from 8 to 10 minutes on each side for well-done steaks. Serves 4 to 6.

Horse-Radish and Cheese Sandwiches

> 8 *slices whole wheat bread*
> ½ *cup butter*
> ½ *cup mild spreading cheese*
> 4 *teaspoons fresh grated or bottled*
>   *horse-radish*

Spread bread with butter, top with cheese and top cheese with horse-radish. Butter each side and toast. Serve with baked beans. Makes 8 sandwiches.

Apple Ale

> ½ *cup sugar*
> 1 *cup water*
> 18 *sprigs apple mint*
> 4 *lemons*
> 1 *quart ginger ale*

Boil sugar and water until sugar is dissolved. Remove from heat and add 10 sprigs apple mint. Chill. Add the juice of 4 lemons and strain. After filling mint julep glasses with crushed ice, add ½ cup apple ale and fill to top with ginger ale. Add sprig of apple mint and serve. Serves 4.

Minted Cucumber Conserve

> 1 *cup peeled, diced cucumbers*
> ¾ *cup crushed canned pineapple*
> ¾ *cup lemon juice*
> ¾ *cup apple juice*
> 5 *cups sugar*
> 4 *drops green food colouring*
> 1½ *teaspoons mint flavouring*
> 1 *bottle fruit pectin*
> ½ *cup chopped walnuts*

Combine cucumbers, pineapple, lemon juice, apple juice, and sugar in large kettle. Stir well and bring to full rolling boil for 1 minute, stirring constantly. Add colouring and mint flavouring. Remove from heat. Stir in pectin, skim, and stir for 5 minutes. Add walnuts. Put in scalded jars or glasses and cover with ⅛ inch hot paraffin. Makes 8 8-ounce glasses. Serve with lamb.

Universal Mint Sauce

> ½ *cup chopped mint*
> ⅔ *cup mild white vinegar*
> 3 *tablespoons sugar*

Wash mint before stripping leaves from the stalks. Dry thoroughly, chop finely, and add vinegar and sugar. Put in a crockery jar and let stand overnight. Be sure sugar is dissolved. Serve with roast leg of lamb.

Pickled Nasturtium Pods

> 1 *pint nasturtium pods*
> 1 *clove bud*
> 1 *allspice bud*
> ¼ *teaspoon mace*
> 1 *tablespoon olive oil*
> ½ *teaspoon freshly grated horse-radish*
> 2 *cups mild white vinegar*
> ¼ *teaspoon salt*

Pick only plump, green, well-filled nasturtium pods. Wash and set aside. Place clove, allspice, mace, olive oil, and horse-radish in pottery container; heat vinegar and salt. Then add pods to spices. Pour vinegar over all ingredients and let marinate for 24 hours. Use as you would use capers over stuffed tomatoes or sea-food salads.

Orégano Pork Mexicana

> 2 *pounds fresh pork tenderloin*
> 1 *clove garlic*
> ½ *teaspoon orégano*
> ½ *cup salad oil*
> ½ *cup ripe olives*
> ½ *cup seedless raisins*
> ½ *cup green peppers*
> 1 *cup tomato purée*
> 2 *teaspoons salt*
> 1 *teaspoon chili powder*
> ¼ *teaspoon cayenne pepper*
> 2 *tablespoons flour*
> 2 *cups water*
> ½ *teaspoon cumin seed*

Rub pork tenderloin with crushed garlic and orégano. Brown pork on each side in salad oil. Slice ripe olives, then add to the pork with raisins, green peppers, tomato purée, salt, chili powder, and cayenne pepper. Mix flour in ¾ cup water, stir into pork pan gently. Add remaining water and stir until smooth. Put into oven and bake until pork is tender. Before serving sprinkle generously with cumin seed. Serves 4 to 6.

Parsley Broiled Fillets

> 12 *fish fillets*
> 2 *cups milk*
> 12 *tiny white onions*
> 12 *fresh mushrooms*
> 1 *green pepper*
> 8 *tablespoons butter*
> 2 *tablespoons flour*
> 1 *pint heavy cream*
> ¼ *teaspoon white pepper*
> ½ *teaspoon paprika*
> ½ *cup chopped fresh parsley*

Poach fillets in 1 cup milk until tender and set aside. Cook onions, mushrooms, and green pepper in 2 teaspoons butter until tender. Make white sauce with 4 tablespoons butter, 2 tablespoons flour, 1 cup milk, and 1 pint cream. Flake fillets. Put onions, mushrooms, and green pepper in a well-greased casserole, then add flaked fillets and white sauce. Dot with remaining butter, sprinkle with pepper, paprika, and parsley. Place under the broiler until the top is a golden brown. A delightful dish with a velvet touch!

PARSLEY PARTY PÂTÉ

> 1 *envelope plain gelatin*
> 1 *can beef consommé (undiluted)*
> 2 *cans liver pâté*
> ¼ *teaspoon minced garlic*
> ½ *teaspoon Worcestershire sauce*
> 2 *teaspoons chopped parsley*

Dissolve gelatin in warm consommé by placing saucepan over low heat and stirring until gelatin is completely dissolved. Pour into small mould or bowl and chill in the refrigerator until set—about 2 hours. Combine pâté, garlic, Worcestershire, and parsley. Remove bowl of gelatin from refrigerator and scoop out centre of gelatin, leaving about ¼ inch gelatin around sides and on bottom. Put gelatin in saucepan. Pack pâté mixture carefully into mould. Melt gelatin removed from the mould over low heat; cool and pour over top of pâté; chill until completely firm. To unmould, set bowl in warm water briefly to loosen, invert plate over top, then turn. Serve with crackers. Garnish with ripe olives, radish roses, carrot sticks, and water cress. Scrumptious!

ENCHILADAS KELSAZ

> 4 *fresh eggs*
> 3 *tablespoons oil*
> 1 *cup milk*
> 1 *cup flour*
> 1 *teaspoon baking powder*

Put all ingredients into blender and buzz until blended. Pour on well-greased hot griddle. Cook one large enchilada at a time until golden brown.

FILLING FOR ENCHILADAS KELSAZ

$\frac{1}{2}$ *cup olive oil*
2 *cups ground lean pork*
$\frac{1}{2}$ *cup minced onions*
$\frac{1}{4}$ *teaspoon pepper*
1 *cup tomatoes*
$\frac{1}{2}$ *teaspoon cayenne pepper*
$\frac{1}{2}$ *teaspoon marjoram*
$\frac{1}{2}$ *teaspoon salt*
1 *tablespoon paprika*
1 *teaspoon chili powder*
1 *cup grated cheese*

Put oil in large heavy skillet and heat. Add lean pork; cook to a light brown. Remove from skillet and drain on paper towel. Reheat oil in skillet, put in onions, pepper, tomatoes, cayenne pepper, marjoram, salt, paprika, and chili powder. Cook until thick. Put a spoonful of pork, a spoonful of cheese, and a spoonful of chili mixture on enchiladas. Roll up as you would a jelly roll. Serve hot.

RED PEPPER POT SOUP

1 *beef bone*
3 *quarts water*
$\frac{1}{2}$ *pound ground beef*
$2\frac{1}{2}$ *onions, chopped*
$\frac{3}{4}$ *cup carrots, shredded*
2 *large white potatoes, cut in cubes*
$\frac{1}{2}$ *cup finely chopped celery*
$\frac{1}{3}$ *box spaghetti*
$\frac{1}{2}$ *cup green peas*
$\frac{1}{2}$ *can tomatoes (No. 2)*
1 *teaspoon thyme*
1 *tablespoon salt*
$\frac{1}{4}$ *teaspoon red peppers, chopped*
$\frac{1}{2}$ *teaspoon black pepper*
$\frac{3}{4}$ *teaspoon paprika*

Cook beef bone 1 hour in 3 quarts water. Add ground beef, onions, carrots, potatoes, and celery, and let simmer $2\frac{1}{2}$ hours. Add spaghetti, peas, and tomatoes. Add remaining ingredients and simmer ½ hour. Serves 6.

RED DEVIL SQUASH CREOLE

6 *medium or small summer squashes*
3 *tablespoons butter*
2 *medium onions, sliced*
1 *large green pepper, cut in strips*
3 *tablespoons brown sugar*
3 *tablespoons flour*
1 *quart fresh tomatoes, quartered*
Salt to taste
Red pepper (some like it hot,
     others hotter)
¼ *pound sharp cheese*

Cook squash until tender, drain off excess liquid. Put butter into a large skillet, add onion rings and pepper strips, and cook over low heat until tender. Sprinkle brown sugar over onion and peppers, add flour, turn gently. Arrange tomato quarters over all and simmer a few minutes. In well-buttered casserole or baking dish, put a layer of squash, a layer of tomato mixture, another layer of squash, and so on. Salt and red pepper to taste. Top with grated sharp cheese. Bake at 350° F. until cheese is well browned, about 30 minutes. Serves 6 to 8.

ACCENT ON CHILI

5 *onions, chopped*
2 *green peppers, chopped*
2 *pounds lean ground beef*
2 *tablespoons bacon fat*
2 *pint cans tomatoes*
¼ *teaspoon pepper*
1 *teaspoon salt*
⅛ *teaspoon cayenne pepper*
2 *whole cloves*
1 *bay leaf*
1 *tablespoon chili powder*
1 *large can kidney beans*

Cook onions, green peppers, and beef on low heat in bacon fat for 30 minutes. Stir often. Cook until onions and peppers are tender. Add tomatoes and all seasonings. Simmer very slowly for 30 minutes, add beans, and serve hot. Serves 6.

Party Pic-a-unes

> 1 *package Triskets*
> 1 *package Rice Chex*
> 1 *package Wheat Chex*
> 1 *small box pretzels*
> 1 *tablespoon seasoning salt*
> 1 *teaspoon marjoram*
> 1 *teaspoon savory*
> ½ *teaspoon garlic powder*
> ½ *teaspoon onion powder*
> ¼ *teaspoon cayenne pepper*
> ½ *stick butter*

Place all ingredients except butter in a large baking dish. Cut butter in pieces and dot entire top surface. Place in preheated oven, 250° F., mix gently. Serve hot. Serves 12.

Red Rhubarb Parfait Pie

> 1 *baked pie shell*
> ½ *cup sugar*
> 4 *cups rhubarb, cut in 1-inch sections*
> 2 *cups water*
> *gelatin or other thickener*
> 1 *pint vanilla ice cream*
> ½ *pint heavy cream*
> 1 *cup strawberries*

For filling, combine sugar, rhubarb, and ½ cup water; cook over very low heat to a saucelike consistency. Heat 1½ cups water to boiling, add gelatin, which has been dissolved in ¼ cup cold water, and stir until gelatin is completely dissolved. Chill, then add ice cream. Fold cooled rhubarb into ice cream-gelatin mixture. Pour into a baked pie shell. Chill in refrigerator until time to serve. Top with whipped cream. Decorate with whole strawberries. Lovely, luscious, and unforgettable.

Ruby-Red Rhubarb Punch

>2 *pounds rhubarb*
>3 *cups water*
>2 *lemons, sliced thin*
>1¾ *cups sugar*
>1 *cup orange juice*
>1 *large square ice*
>2 *quarts carbonated water*

Wash and cut rhubarb in inch-long pieces, cook with the water and lemon slices about 20 minutes. Strain and add sugar; stir until dissolved. When chilled, add orange juice. Place ice in punch bowl. Combine punch and carbonated water and pour over ice. Serve. Colourful and sparkling. Serves 8.

Rosemary Mediterranean Soup

>5-*pound hen*
>2 *quarts water*
>2 *carrots*
>1 *onion*
>3 *celery tops*
>6 *sprigs parsley*
>1 *bay leaf*
>3 *whole cloves*
>1 *tablespoon salt*
>¼ *teaspoon pepper*
>½ *teaspoon rosemary*
>2 *tablespoons tapioca*

Cook hen in 2 quarts water until meat falls off the bones (save the meat for chicken salad). Strain chicken broth, add diced carrots, sliced onion, celery tops, parsley, bay leaf, cloves, salt, pepper, and rosemary. Simmer until carrots and onions are tender. Strain, cool, skim off fat. Add 2 tablespoons quick-cooking tapioca. Heat thoroughly, serve with shredded hard-boiled eggs, strips of pimiento, or whipped cream passed separately for garnishes. Serves 6 to 8.

SAVORY TAMALE PIE

> 1½ *pounds ground beef chuck*
> ½ *pound lean pork*
> 2 *large cans pitted ripe olives* (*black*)
> 1 *quart or* 1 *pound mushrooms*
> 3 *small cans tomato purée*
> 6 *or less dried red peppers, or red pepper*
>   (some like it HOT!)
> 1 *teaspoon dried savory*
> 3 *cups corn meal lots and lots of butter*

Combine beef and pork and sauté in large skillet. Stir to keep large chunks from forming. Slice ripe olives and cut mushrooms in small slices. Now get a large kettle. Open the tomato purée and dilute with water to a semi-thick paste. Break up red peppers into this, add meat, olives, mushrooms, and savory, and simmer for 15 minutes. It should be thick but *not dry*.

SAVORY POTATOES

> 4 *large potatoes*
> 2 *large onions*
> ½ *teaspoon salt*
> ¼ *teaspoon pepper*
> 2 *tablespoons butter*
> 1 *teaspoon savory*
> 2 *cups milk*

Peel and slice potatoes and onions very thin. Prepare a well-buttered casserole. Put in a layer of potatoes, a layer of onions, salt, pepper, butter, and a sprinkling of savory. Add another layer of potatoes, onions, and seasonings. Pour milk over all, cover, and bake at 350° F. until tender. Add more milk if needed. Serves 6.

'OPEN SESAME' COOKIES

$\frac{3}{4}$ *cups shortening*
1 *cup sugar*
2 *fresh eggs*
$\frac{1}{4}$ *teaspoon almond extract*
$\frac{1}{4}$ *teaspoon lemon extract*
2 *tablespoons sweet cream*
$2\frac{1}{2}$ *cups flour*
$\frac{1}{2}$ *teaspoon baking soda*
$\frac{1}{4}$ *teaspoon salt*
$\frac{1}{4}$ *cup finely chopped almonds*
$\frac{1}{4}$ *cup sesame seeds*

Cream shortening and sugar. Beat until fluffy. Add the unbeaten eggs, one at a time, beat thoroughly. Combine flavouring and cream and add. Sift flour, soda, and salt together. Add to first mixture and blend well. Add chopped almonds and sesame seeds, then chill in refrigerator overnight. When ready to bake, roll out thin on lightly floured board and cut with large cooky cutter. Place on ungreased cooky sheet. Garnish with whole almond in centre, sprinkle tops with sesame seeds. Bake at 375° F. about 10 minutes. Yields $2\frac{1}{2}$ dozen.

NOTE: I often use a large doughnut cutter and sprinkle all over with sesame seeds. The small cooky from the centre may be garnished with a whole almond.

TARRAGON TASTYS

6 *slices bread*
3 *tablespoons melted butter*
1 *cup grated or spreading cheese*
1 *teaspoon tarragon, chopped*
6 *slices boiled ham*

Brush a slice of bread with melted butter, spread generously with cheese, sprinkle with tarragon, and top with a slice of boiled ham. Continue until you have 6 tarragon tastys. Place on cooky sheet and broil in the oven until cheese is golden brown. Serve with broiled tomatoes on the side. Pass bread and butter pickles. Serves 3.

ENGLISH THYME STUFFING
For 2 2-pound broilers

> 3 *tablespoons minced onion*
> 3 *tablespoons butter*
> ½ *cup chopped mushrooms*
> ½ *pound chicken livers*
> ½ *teaspoon salt*
> ¼ *teaspoon pepper*
> ½ *teaspoon marjoram*
> ½ *teaspoon thyme*

Sauté minced onion in butter, add mushrooms, cook slowly until tender. Add diced chicken livers, salt, pepper, marjoram, and thyme. Cook over low heat until chicken livers are tender. Force through a potato ricer until well blended. Split broilers that have been broiled and stuff each half with thyme stuffing. Cover with buttered crumbs, return to broiler until buttered crumbs are a golden brown. Place on platter, garnish with parsley. Serves 4.

WHITE PEPPER POTATO SOUP
'par excellence'

> 4 *large potatoes*
> 2 *large onions*
> ½ *teaspoon salt*
> 1¼ *cups water*
> 1 *quart milk*
> 1 *pint heavy cream*
> 3 *tablespoons flour*
> ¼ *pound butter*
> ½ *teaspoon white pepper*
> ½ *teaspoon paprika*

Peel and cube potatoes and onions. Add salt and 1 cup water (hold ¼ cup), simmer until tender. Drain off water, add milk and cream. Mix flour and ¼ cup cold water to a thin smooth paste, add to soup, and simmer on low heat until thickened. Pour into cream soup bowls. Cut butter into 8 cubes and add 1 cube to each soup bowl. Sprinkle *generously* with white pepper and garnish with paprika. Serves 8.

BLACK-SEEDED SIMPSON SALAD

½ gallon garden lettuce leaves
4 crisp green onions
4 fresh eggs
3 tablespoons bacon drippings
2 tablespoons brown sugar
½ teaspoon salt
¼ teaspoon red pepper
¼ teaspoon black pepper
¾ cup cider vinegar
¼ cup water

Wash and crisp lettuce leaves. Slice onions in thin slices, green tops and all. The eggs should be hard-boiled and set aside. Line a large wooden salad bowl with one layer of frilled lettuce, leaving a ruffle of leaves above the top of the bowl. Tear lettuce in chunks (by hand), add a layer of lettuce, onion slices, boiled egg slices—layer on layer until bowl is filled. Garnish with egg slices.

DRESSING: Heat heavy iron skillet. Add bacon drippings, brown sugar, salt, red pepper, black pepper, vinegar, and water and simmer 1 minute. Pour hot dressing over salad. Cover with a large plate to keep steam in. Appetizing and delicious. Serves 6.

BEAU BRUMMELL POMANDERS

Traditional spice-scented pomanders are quaint and delightful to hang in cupboards the year round.

2 small thin-skinned oranges
1 box powdered cinnamon
1 small box powdered orris root
1 box powdered angelica root
2 large boxes whole cloves

Mix cinnamon, orris root, and angelica. Use fork with sharp tines to make holes all over oranges. Put cloves into each hole. Roll clove-covered oranges in mixed spices and let stand overnight. Roll again in spices until no moisture shows. Stand on paper towels for about a week and dust frequently with spices.

THELMA'S CLOVE PICKLE
Watermelon Rind

> 10 *pounds watermelon rind*
> 1 *quart sugar*
> 1 *quart white vinegar*
> 40 *drops oil of cinnamon*
> 40 *drops oil of cloves*

Peel, cut, wash, and cover rind with cold water for 24 hours. Second day, drain and rewash. Cover with cold water and simmer for 10 minutes. Drain, cover again with cold water, and drain. Put rind in kettle, add sugar, vinegar, and oils. Colour with green vegetable colour and stir often for 3 days. Bring to a boil and allow to boil for 10 minutes after it starts to bubble. Put in jars or crocks. Not necessary to seal.

EARLY AMERICAN HOT BUTTERED RUM
Great Winter Warmer

> 2 *ounces Puerto Rican or other rum*
> 1 *teaspoon sugar*
> 1 *stick cinnamon*
> *pinch of nutmeg*

Place ingredients in preheated mug. Fill with boiling water. Drop in generous blob of butter. Dip a cube of sugar in rum and light. Float flaming cube on top. Relax before open fire.
Drink!

CINNAMON CRÈME DE BANANES

> 2 *bananas*
> 4 *tablespoons butter*
> $\frac{3}{4}$ *cup brown sugar*
> 1 *teaspoon cinnamon*
> 1 *ounce rum*
> $\frac{1}{2}$ *ounce crème de bananes*

Our Latin-American friends start this luscious dessert by peeling 2 bananas and then cutting them into 4 strips. In a large pan, so as not to crowd bananas, melt the butter, add brown sugar and cinnamon. When the sugar has melted and the mixture begins to thicken, place bananas in the pan and cook until soft. Remove from fire, add rum and crème de bananes. Ignite and serve while hot. Serves 4. A perfect dessert with your coffee.

TRADITIONAL EGGNOG

> 6 *fresh eggs*
> ¾ *cup sugar*
> 1 *pint heavy cream*
> 1 *pint milk*
> 1 *pint straight bourbon*
> 1 *ounce Jamaica rum*
> *ground nutmeg*

Beat egg yolks separately. Add ½ cup sugar to yolks. Beat egg whites very stiff. Add ¼ cup sugar to egg whites. Fold in cream, milk, bourbon, and rum. Serve very cold with grated nutmeg on the top of each cup. Makes 5 pints.

MACE SAUCE FOR FRUIT DISHES

> 1 *cup sugar*
> 2 *tablespoons cornflour*
> ¼ *teaspoon salt*
> 1 *teaspoon mace*
> 2 *cups water*
> 2 *tablespoons butter*

Blend sugar, cornflour, salt, and mace. Add water and cook over low heat until thick and clear. Add butter. Serve over fruit rolls, pie, or pudding.

MACE MEXICAN WEDDING CAKES
by Sally

> ½ *cup butter*
> 1 *teaspoon vanilla*
> ½ *cup sugar*
> 2 *cups sifted flour*
> 1 *teaspoon mace*
> 1 *cup chopped walnuts*
> 6 *tablespoons icing sugar*

Cream butter, vanilla, and sugar. Stir in flour, mace, and chopped nuts. Mix well. Drop small balls on well-greased cooky sheet. Bake 10 to 12 minutes at 400° F. Remove from oven and roll in confectioners' sugar while still warm. Store overnight before serving. Makes 3 to 4 dozen cakes.

ALLSPICE WASSAIL BOWL

> 1 *gallon apple cider*
> 1 *cup dark brown sugar (packed)*
> 1 *can frozen lemon juice concentrate*
> 1 *can frozen orange juice concentrate*
> 1 *tablespoon whole cloves*
> 1 *tablespoon allspice*
> 1 *tablespoon ground nutmeg*
> 24 *cinnamon sticks*

In large kettle, combine cider, brown sugar, undiluted lemon juice, and undiluted orange juice. Tie cloves and allspice in cheese-cloth. Add to cider along with nutmeg. Cover and simmer for 20 minutes. Remove and discard clove bag. Serve hot in mugs with a cinnamon stick in each mug. Makes 24 mugs.

BETH'S SPICE CAKE

> 1 *cup butter*
> 2 *cups sugar*
> 4 *large eggs*
> 1½ *cups applesauce*
> 3 *cups sifted cake flour*
> 1½ *teaspoons soda*
> ½ *teaspoon ginger*
> ½ *teaspoon cloves*
> ½ *teaspoon allspice*
> 2 *squares unsweetened chocolate*

Cream butter and sugar. Add eggs and applesauce. Sift flour, soda, and all the spices together, and add gradually to cake mixture. Melt chocolate over hot water and add to cake for a lovely rich colour. Makes 3 large 9-inch layers. Bake at 375° F. for 20 minutes. Ice with mocha icing.

Mocha Icing

> 1 *box confectioners' sugar*
> ⅛ *stick butter*
> ½ *cup strong black coffee*

Put sugar into a large mixing bowl. Melt butter and gradually add coffee and melted butter alternately until mixture is the right spreading consistency. Ice tops and sides of cake and decorate with English or black walnut halves. Luscious and lovely!

All-spiced Blueberry Pie

> 1 *cup sugar*
> 2 *tablespoons tapioca*
> ¼ *teaspoon cinnamon*
> ¼ *teaspoon cloves*
> ¼ *teaspoon allspice*
> 4 *cups freshly picked blueberries*

Mix sugar, tapioca, cinnamon, cloves, and allspice and mix with blueberries in a large bowl.

Pastry

Prepare pastry for a double-crust pie:

> 1½ *cups flour*
> ½ *teaspoon salt*
> ½ *teaspoon baking powder*
> ½ *cup cooking fat or oil*
> 4 *tablespoons cold water*

Sift flour, salt, and baking powder together. Mix in fat. Gradually add cold water to make stiff dough. Chill dough. Cut off enough pastry for the undercrust. Use a 9-inch pan. Roll pastry to about ¼ inch in thickness and a little larger than the pan. Pierce top crust with fork several times. Bake at 450° F. for 30 minutes, then reduce heat and bake 10 minutes longer. Serves 6 to 8.

A Bay-Flavoured Chowder of Lamb Kidneys

½ *pound butter*
12 *medium onions*
12 *lamb kidneys*
¼ *teaspoon paprika*
2 *tablespoons flour*
2 *pints light cream*
¼ *cup dry vermouth*
3 *sprigs fresh parsley*
¼ *teaspoon thyme*
1 *bay leaf*
1 *clove bud*
1 *tablespoon lemon juice*
1 *tablespoon unsalted butter*
½ *teaspoon salt*
¼ *teaspoon pepper*

Put butter into large deep fryer. Slice onions into butter, cook until tender and gold, not brown. Quarter lamb kidneys, add to onions and butter, cook and keep turning for about 5 minutes. Add paprika and flour, stir, and turn gently. Pour 1 pint cream over kidneys and onions, add vermouth, parsley, thyme, bay leaf, clove bud. Cover and simmer about 30 minutes. Add the other pint of cream during the cooking period. When done add lemon juice, 1 tablespoon sweet butter, and salt and pepper. The chowder should be thin like oyster stew. Serve piping hot. Serves 6.

Ginger 'n' Honey Crumb Cake

3 *cups sifted cake flour*
1 *teaspoon salt*
½ *teaspoon soda*
½ *teaspoon baking powder*
½ *teaspoon ground cloves*
1 *teaspoon ground ginger*
½ *cup cooking fat or oil*
1 *cup sugar*
1 *cup boiling water*

Herbal Recipes

1 *cup strained honey*
½ *cup thin strips crystallized or*
candied ginger

Sift together flour, salt, soda, baking powder, and spices. Combine with shortening and sugar. Mix to a crumbling consistency. Set aside ½ cup crumbs for top of cake. Combine boiling water and honey. Add to the rest of the crumb mixture, beat until smooth. Sprinkle the half cup of crumbs over the top. Bake in loaf pan at 375° F. for about 40 minutes. Decorate top of cake with the thin sliced candied ginger while the cake is still hot. Serves 8.

GINGER-TOMATO PRESERVES

2 *pounds ripe tomatoes*
2 *pounds cooking apples*
6 *cups sugar*
½ *teaspoon salt*
2 *lemons (medium)*
2 *cups water*
1 *cup seedless raisins*
1 *cup chopped walnuts*
¼ *cup chopped candied ginger*

Scald and peel tomatoes, cut in very small pieces, and place in large kettle. Peel and core apples, cut in small pieces, and add to tomatoes. Add sugar and salt. Stir over medium heat until sugar dissolves. Simmer until mixture thickens. Cook until fruit is transparent and syrup is thick. Slice lemons very thin, remove seeds, cut each slice in eight sections, and add water. Cook over medium heat until rind is very tender. Add to tomatoes. Add raisins, walnuts, and ginger and cook about 15 minutes longer. Pack in scalded jars at once, and cover with ¼-inch layer hot paraffin. Serve with pork dinners. For holiday gifts, wrap and tie with red ribbon bow.

Christmas Cardamom Cake

> 1 *cup sugar*
> ½ *cup melted butter*
> 4 *eggs, well beaten*
> 4 *cups sifted cake flour*
> *pinch of salt*
> 4 *teaspoons baking powder*
> ½ *cup milk*
> 1½ *cups chopped dates*
> 1½ *cups chopped cherries, orange and*
>   *lemon peel*
> ½ *teaspoon ground cardamom seed*

Bake Christmas cake as the sun rises. If you wait until sunset cake will be sad.

Combine sugar, butter, and eggs. Beat until smooth. Sift together flour, salt, and baking powder. Add alternately with milk to first mixture. Add dates, fruit peel, and cardamom seeds. Fold in thoroughly. Pour into well-greased pound cake pan, bake at 325° F. about 1½ hours.

Cardamom-Flavoured Grape Pie

> 4 *cups grapes*
> ¾ *cup sugar*
> ⅛ *teaspoon cardamom seed*
> 1 *tablespoon tapioca (quick-cooking*
>   *if available)*
> 1 *tablespoon grated orange rind*
> ½ *teaspoon lemon juice*
> *pastry for 2-crust pie*
> *whipped cream*

Stew grapes and slip the pulp out of the skins; set skins aside and cook pulp until seeds loosen. Remove seeds and combine pulp, skins, sugar, cardamom seed, tapioca, orange rind, and lemon juice. Pour into a 9-inch pastry-lined pan and cover with old-fashioned pastry lattice. Bake about 30 minutes at 375° F. and serve warm with whipped cream.

Deep South Ice Cream

> 3 *pints light cream*
> 1 *cup sugar*
> *pinch of salt*
> 2 *fresh eggs, beaten*
> 2 *teaspoons vanilla extract*

Scald cream in double boiler. Add sugar, salt, and eggs. Cool, then add vanilla extract. Freeze in hand-turned freezer, using 8 parts ice, 1 part coarse salt. Makes 2 quarts.

Vanilla Icebox Cake

> 1 *stick butter*
> 1 *cup powdered sugar*
> 3 *egg yolks, beaten*
> 1 *teaspoon vanilla extract*
> 1½ *ounces unsweetened chocolate,*
>   *melted*
> ½ *cup coconut flakes*
> ½ *cup chopped pecans*
> 6-*ounce package vanilla wafers, crushed*
> 3 *stiffly-beaten egg whites*
> 1 *cup heavy cream, whipped*
> 2 *tablespoons powdered sugar*
> ½ *teaspoon vanilla extract*

Cream butter and sugar together, add egg yolks and 1 teaspoon vanilla extract. Add chocolate, coconut, pecans, and vanilla wafers. Fold in egg whites and pack in buttered baking dish, 3 by 8 by 10 inches. Chill in refrigerator overnight. Top with whipped cream that has been sweetened with the 2 tablespoons powdered sugar and flavoured with ½ teaspoon vanilla extract. Delicious! Serves 9.

Floating Island

> 3 *eggs, separated*
> 6 *tablespoons sugar*
> ¼ *teaspoon salt*
> 2½ *cups milk*
> ¼ *cup sugar*
> 2 *tablespoons cornflour*
> ¼ *teaspoon salt*
> ½ *teaspoon vanilla extract*
> ¼ *teaspoon almond extract*
> *dash of nutmeg*
> 2 *cups well-drained fruit*

Beat egg whites until stiff. Gradually add the 6 tablespoons sugar and ¼ teaspoon salt, beating until mixture holds its shape. Pour milk into 10-inch skillet; heat. Drop egg-white mixture on milk by table-spoonfuls; cook in simmering milk until set. Carefully remove meringues to tray. Cool at room temperature, then refrigerate.

Strain milk—there should be 2 cups. Combine ¼ cup sugar, corn-flour, and ¼ teaspoon salt. Gradually add milk. Cook in double boiler over hot water, stirring until slightly thickened. Beat egg yolks; add to hot mixture gradually. Cook over hot water, stirring until mixture coats spoon. Cool, add vanilla extract, almond extract, and nutmeg. Chill before serving. Serve with meringues on top and add fresh fruit or berries. Serves 6 to 8.

Orange Jiffy Gems

> 1 *box cake mix*
> ½ *cup fresh orange juice*
> 1 *egg, unbeaten*
> ½ *teaspoon vanilla extract*

Stir ¼ cup orange juice into mix and beat 150 strokes by hand. Add egg and beat 75 strokes. Stir in remaining juice and vanilla extract and beat 75 strokes.

Grease doll-size muffin pans generously. Dust with sifted corn-starch. Fill pans barely half full. Bake at 350° F. about 15 minutes, or until a delicate brown. Remove gems from pan, cool. Insert fork into gem and dip bottom side into ORANGE SYRUP. Hold gem over pan until excess syrup drops off. Place gems on wax paper to drain. Store in airtight tins. Delicious to serve with COFFEE ROYALE.

ORANGE SYRUP

> 1 *cup fresh orange juice*
> 2 *cups sugar*
> 2 *tablespoons grated orange rind*

Combine orange juice, sugar, and orange rind in deep saucepan. Stir over low heat until sugar is dissolved. Boil until you have a thick syrup.

CURRIED LAMB WITH MACARONI

> 1 *pound lamb, cubed*
> ½ *pound macaroni*
> 2 *tablespoons butter*
> 2 *tablespoons flour*
> 2 *tablespoons curry powder*
> 1 *teaspoon salt*
> ¼ *teaspoon pepper*
> 2 *cups milk*

Sauté cubes of lamb in butter. Cover and steam until tender. Cook macaroni in boiling salted water until done. Drain. In a saucepan melt 2 tablespoons butter, add flour, curry powder, salt, and pepper, and blend thoroughly. Add milk gradually, stirring constantly, and cook until a smooth slightly thick sauce results. In casserole put alternate layers of macaroni, lamb, and curry sauce. Repeat until all is used. Cover and bake at 350° F. for 45 minutes. Serves 4.

TURMERIC GARDEN SALAD

> 1 *head green cabbage*
> 4 *large white onions*
> 2 *green sweet peppers*
> 2 *red sweet peppers*
> 1 *bunch bleached celery*

Chop cabbage and slice onions in thin rings. Cut peppers in thin strips about 1 inch long. Dice celery. Put in large salad bowl and chill.

TURMERIC DRESSING

> 2 *cups sugar*
> 2 *cups mild white vinegar*
> 1 *tablespoon salt*
> 1 *teaspoon celery salt*
> 4 *tablespoons flour*
> 1 *teaspoon turmeric*

Combine above ingredients and cook, stirring until thickened. May be served as a *hot* dressing over the garden salad or stored and chilled. Serves 8.

SAFFRON RICE AND CHICKEN

> 2 *frying chickens*
> 1 *cup olive oil*
> 1 *onion*
> 2 *cloves garlic*
> 1 *6-ounce can tomatoes*
> 6 *cups water*
> 1 *bay leaf*
> 2 *teaspoons salt*
> 2 *cups rice*
> $\frac{1}{4}$ *teaspoon saffron*
> 1 *green pepper*
> 1 *2-ounce can petits pois (small green peas)*
> 2 *pimentos*

Cut chicken into pieces and fry in olive oil in large Dutch oven. Add onion and garlic. When tender, add tomatoes and water and simmer for 5 minutes, then add bay leaf, salt, rice, saffron, and green pepper. Stir carefully and bake at 350° F. for 20 minutes. Serve piping hot, garnished with petits pois and pimentos. Serves 6.

CAPERS CRAB MEAT SALAD

6 *medium tomatoes*
⅓ *cup French dressing*
2 *cups flaked crab meat*
½ *cup diced celery*
6 *tablespoons mayonnaise*
¼ *cup capers*
paprika
water cress

Scald, peel, and chill tomatoes, then hollow out to form cups. Marinate inside of tomatoes with French dressing for 30 minutes. Mix crab meat, celery, and French dressing gently so the crab meat will not be broken. Stuff tomatoes and garnish with mayonnaise capers, and paprika. Place on crystal salad plates on a bed of water cress. Piquant flavour with a flourish. Serves 6.

YAM CRISPS

4 *medium yams*
½ *cup brown sugar*
½ *cup zwieback crumbs*
¼ *teaspoon ground capsicum*
½ *cup butter*

Cook yams in their jackets, cool, peel, and cut in strips 1 by 2 inches. Mix brown sugar, zwieback crumbs, and capsicum. Dredge yam strips. Fry to a crisp light brown in butter. Watch and turn often as they burn easily. Serve hot. Serves 2. If you have no zwieback, use melba toast crumbs, dry and crisp.

PAPRIKA BUTTER

6 *tablespoons butter*
½ *teaspoon onion powder*
1 *teaspoon paprika*
¼ *cup chopped chives*

Sauté onion powder in 2 tablespoons butter until a golden brown. Cool and add paprika. Cream the remaining butter and add. Shape into balls and roll in chopped chives. Use on broiled fish, poultry, or baked potatoes.

THE DRINK OF THE GODS

Hot chocolate à la Mexicano is made from the black buttery squares created just for the drink. The woman of Tehuantepec mixes it in a tall gourd (*jicara*) with a whirling stick that acts like a churn in her deft hands. Into the *jicara* go the chocolate, a cup of hot water, sugar or honey, nutmeg, and an egg. Whirling and whirling, the whole becomes a foamy liquid delight. It is served to you in a carved gourd bowl, dark and rich but not too sweet. Once, for the Aztec and Mayan rulers, it was served in solid gold chalices with tortoise-shell and mother-of-pearl spoons.

English cocoa is very sweet and milky, with a dust of nutmeg on top. The French make a more savoury chocolate by using cream, rum, cinnamon, or nutmeg. The Swiss make it with milk and vanilla. Americans like a rich cocoa, or hot chocolate, made with milk and a float of whipped cream on top.

POT DE CRÈME

3 *squares unsweetened chocolate*
1 *teaspoon water*
6 *egg yolks*
3 *tablespoons sugar*
3 *cups heavy cream*
2 *tablespoons crème de cacao*

Melt chocolate in water. Add well-beaten egg yolks and sugar to cream; add crème de cacao to mixture. Blend with melted chocolate slowly. Strain into cups. Place cups in pan of warm water and bake at 300° F. until set. Serves 6.

CHOCOLATE SAUCE

½ *pound unsweetened chocolate*
2 *cups sugar*
pinch of salt
1 *can evaporated milk*
1 *teaspoon vanilla*

Put chocolate, sugar, and salt in double boiler and cook 45 minutes, stirring occasionally. Add the milk and cook another half hour. Cool and add vanilla.

Quickie Cocoa Cake

> 1 *box spongecake mix*
> 1 *pint heavy cream*
> ⅔ *cup instant cocoa*
> ½ *cup icing sugar*
> ⅓ *cup chocolate shot (cake decorations)*

Make cake according to directions on the box. Bake cake in loaf or funnel cake pan and cool. Whip cream, not too stiff, add cocoa and sugar. Ice cake all over. Sprinkle chocolate shot over top of cake to decorate.

Quaint Perfumed Salt Beads

> 2 *tablespoons cornflour*
> ¼ *cup eau de cologne or toilet water*
> 3 *drops food colouring*
> ½ *cup table salt*

Mix cornflour, cologne, and food colouring to make a thin paste. Put salt in a heavy skillet, heat to very hot. Add salt to paste, mix and knead it until a thick dough has been formed. Shape small, medium, and large rolls of dough about 3 inches long. Cut off small uniform pieces and shape into balls. Put a toothpick through each ball or bead and stand pick in a block of styrofoam. Let stand overnight until beads are dry. String on elastic thread or dental floss. Experiment with different colours of food colouring for interesting effects.

Fragrant Victorian Rose Petal Beads can be made by putting 2 quarts of fresh rose petals in a bowl. Twist and crush the petals into a pulp. Dye the pulp with food colouring or, to obtain black beads, spread the pulp in an iron skillet and let stand overnight. Turn frequently so every part comes in contact with the iron surface. While the pulp is moist, shape and string as you would the salt beads.

Beads make nice party favours.

MARGARET'S SUGAR TORTE

> *4 eggs*
> *3 cups sugar*
> *8 tablespoons flour*
> *5 teaspoons baking powder*
> *½ teaspoon salt*
> *2 cups chopped tart apples*
> *2 cups chopped pecans or walnuts*
> *2 cups heavy cream, whipped*

Beat whole eggs until very frothy and lemon-coloured. Sift together sugar, flour, baking powder, and salt. Add to eggs, with the apples and nuts. Pour into two well-buttered baking pans about 8 by 12 inches. Bake at 325° F. about 45 minutes or until crusty and brown.

To serve, scoop up with pancake turner (keeping crust side up). Pile on large plate and cover with whipped cream and sprinkling of chopped nuts to garnish. Serves 16.

BEVERAGES

HOT MOCHA JAVA

There is a happy affinity between coffee and chocolate. Hot Mocha Java blends these two fine flavours. Here is enough for a party.

> *4½ measuring cups hot coffee*
> *4½ measuring cups hot cocoa*

Combine equal quantities coffee and cocoa. Serve hot, but do not boil. Pour into cups or mugs and top with marshmallows. Serves 12.

IRISH COFFEE

Irish coffee travelled from Shannon straight to San Francisco, and from there to the rest of the United States.

> *strong black coffee*
> *fine granulated sugar*
> *Irish whisky*
> *slightly whipped cream*

Into a warmed table wineglass, place 2 teaspoons sugar and fill glass about two-thirds full with hot coffee. Mix. Add about 2 tablespoons Irish whisky and top with softly whipped cream. Serves 1.

Coffee with Liqueurs

Coffee has a talent for mixing sociably with a variety of liquors and liqueurs. Begin with strong demitasse coffee and fill the demitasse cup about three-quarters full. Then add a dash of any of the following: white crême de menthe, curaçao, kümmel, anisette, or cointreau. Cognac in demitasse coffee becomes COFFEE ROYALE, but bourbon or rum may also be used.

Café Brûlot Diabolique

No New Orleans visit is complete without dinner at Antoine's. And that dinner won't be complete until you have the spectacular *spécialité de la maison,* café brûlot diabolique:

> 6 *pieces lump sugar*
> 8 *whole cloves*
> 1 *1-inch cinnamon stick*
> 1 *cut-up lemon peel*
> 4 *jiggers cognac*
> 4 *cups hot coffee*

Place all ingredients, except coffee, in chafing dish. Ignite cognac with match and stir ingredients until well blended. After a minute or two slowly pour in the hot coffee and continue to stir. (In winter, heat brandy before using.) Strain into brûlot or demitasse cups. Serves 4.

Coffee Alexander

Here is a short, summery, after-dinner drink that tastes as good as it looks.

> *crème de cacao*
> *strong, ice-cold coffee*
> *whipped cream*

Pour 2 tablespoons crème de cacao in bottom of table wineglass. Fill almost to top with strong, ice-cold coffee. Mix. Float softly whipped cream on top. Serves 1.

SPICY ICED COFFEE

For those who like their cool drinks tall, dark, and handsome, there's nothing more flavourful than spicy iced coffee. If you're calorie-conscious, try drinking it as it is. Otherwise, it's fine with cream and sugar.

> 3 *cups hot, double-strength coffee*
> 2 *cinnamon sticks*
> 4 *cloves*
> 4 *allspice berries*

Pour coffee over spices. Let stand 1 hour. Strain. Pour over ice in tall glasses. Serve with cream and sugar. Serves 4.

COFFEE-GLAZED HAM LOAF

> 2 *pounds lean pork, ground*
> 1 *pound smoked ham, ground*
> 1 *cup soft bread crumbs*
> 2 *eggs*
> ¼ *cup ketchup*
> ½ *teaspoon salt*

Combine all ingredients and shape into loaf. Bake, uncovered, at 325° F. for 2 hours. During last hour baste four times with COFFEE GLAZE. Serves 6 to 8.

COFFEE GLAZE

> 1 *cup firmly packed brown sugar*
> 1 *cup brewed coffee*
> 1 *teaspoon dry mustard*
> 1 *tablespoon mixed pickling spices, tied in cheesecloth*
> 1 *teaspoon vinegar*

Combine all ingredients and bring to boil. Simmer until mixture forms a thick syrup. Remove spice bag.

DANDELION WINE

1 gallon dandelion blossoms
1 gallon boiling water
3 lemons
1 orange
3 tablespoons sugar
3 tablespoons dry yeast

Put blossoms into the boiling water and let stand 24 hours. Cut lemons and orange in thin slices and add to blossom liquid. Add sugar and yeast, then let stand ten days. Strain and put in jugs, but not airtight.

FINA'S 'TALKING LEAVES' TEA

2 lemons
3 oranges
1 quart water
12 cloves
2 cups sugar
2 quarts prepared Oolong tea

Extract juice from lemons and oranges and hold. Bring water to a rolling boil. Add cloves, then add rinds from lemons and oranges. Add sugar and boil 5 minutes. Remove from heat, add lemon and orange juices. Discard lemon and orange rinds before serving. Add the 2 quarts tea. Serve either piping hot or iced. Wonderful for tea parties. Makes 3 quarts.

TEA FROM ANISE

Use ½ teaspoon anise seeds per cup of water. Bring water to a boil, pour over the anise seeds in teapot. Steep for about 5 minutes. Sweeten to taste and serve hot or iced.

Prepare several cups of plain tea and you can have fun alone or in serving your guests by using a different flavouring in each cup. On following page are some flavourings you may want to start with; then use your own imagination.

mint
crystallized ginger or ginger candy
allspice
marjoram
balm (flavour combination of mint and lemon)

Tea is a good base for punch. Treat yourself by trying some of the combinations of tea, spice, and everything nice!

BEVERAGE CHART:
HOW THE BEVERAGES ARE USED

COFFEE

Hot coffee, iced coffee, coffee ice cream, coffee-flavoured toppings for desserts, Mocha icing for cakes, English toffee confections, pies, liqueurs, gravies, breads, candies, cookies.

TEA

Hot tea, iced tea, tea as a base for fruit punches. Hot Russian tea is made with whole cloves, cinnamon, allspice, and sugar; Swiss tea is made by steeping leaves with cinnamon. Try tea with any of the spices or flavourings; also try tea with ginger ale in equal portions and add mint and lemon.

COCOA
and
CHOCOLATE

Breakfast cocoa, hot chocolate, chocolate ice cream, chocolate sauces, chocolate syrup, chocolate puddings, chocolate cakes, candies, chocolate sodas, chocolate sundaes, and anywhere else where perfect bouquet is needed. Puts a new taste in coffee.

5. Some facts about growing herbs

Oh, Adam was a gardener, and God who made him sees,
*   That half a proper gardener's work is done upon his knees,*
So when your work is finished, you can wash your hands and pray
For the Glory of the Garden that it may not pass away!
And the Glory of the Garden it shall never pass away.

RUDYARD KIPLING

There are two lists, one of the perennials and one of the annuals and biennials. Best wishes for good growing, good cooking, and good eating, which, when combined properly, mean 'pleasurable living'.

PERENNIALS

Ambrosia
Angelica
Balm, Lemon
Bergamot
Betony: Wood, Paul's
Burnet
Calamus
Camomile
Catnip
Horehound
Horse-radish
Hyssop
Lavender
Leek
Lemon Verbena
Lovage
Marjoram, Pot

Chicory
Chives
Costmary
Cress: Upland, Water
Dandelion
Feverfew
Garlic
Germander
Hop
Rue
Sage
Santolina: Lavender
    Cotton, Emerald
    Green
Savory, Winter
Shallot
Sorrel, Wood

PERENNIALS

May, Apple
Mint: Apple, Pepper-
    mint, Spearmint
Orégano
Pennyroyal
Rhubarb
Rocambole
Rosemary
Roses: Damask, Provence,
    Eglantine

Sweet Cicely
Sweet Woodruff
Tansy
Tarragon
Thyme
Wild Ginger
Wintergreen
Yarrow

ANNUALS AND BIENNIALS
OR BEST GROWN AS SUCH

Anise
Borage
Caraway
Chervil
Clary
Coriander
Cress, Garden
Cumin
Dill
Fennels
Fennel Flower
Geranium: Rose,
    Lemon
Marigold

Marjoram, Sweet
Mustards: Black,
    White
Nasturtium
Parsley
Peppers: Tabasco,
    Red Chili
Poppy
Savory, Summer
Sesame
Sorrel: French,
    Garden
Sweet Basil

CULTIVATION—GROWTH—HABITS

NAME	FORM USED	When to plant	Depth to sow seed	Spacing of plants	Germination time	Colour of blossom	Height (inches)	TYPE OF PLANT
AMBROSIA *Oke of Cappadocia*	Fresh flower heads	Best to get plants from herb grower		12 inches		Yellowish	24 to 36	Perennial
ANGELICA *Archangelica officinalis*	Fresh tips; stems, and seeds	Sow seed early spring, transplant seedlings early summer, permanently in autumn	¼ to ½ inch loose soil	36 inches	Slow	White to yellow or green	up to 48	Perennial
ANISE *Pimpinella anisum*	Leaves—fresh; seeds—dried	Sow seeds in early spring	½ inch	8 to 12 inches	14 to 18 days	Yellowish white	18 to 24	Annual
BALM, LEMON *Melissa officinalis*	Leaves—fresh; leaves—dried for potpourri	Propagation by root division or cuttings spring or fall		18 inches		White or purple	18 to 24	Perennial
BERGAMOT *Monarda didyma*	Flowers for arrangements; leaves—fresh	Early spring root division		18 inches		Red	24 to 36	Perennial
BETONY (WOOD) *Betonica officinalis*	Leaves—fresh	Sow seeds or set plants in spring	¼ inch	6 to 8 inches	Slow	White, purple or red	6 to 18	Perennial

HERB GROWING CHART

NAME	FORM USED	CULTIVATION—GROWTH—HABITS						TYPE OF PLANT
		When to plant	*Depth to sow seed*	*Spacing of plants*	*Germination time*	*Colour of blossom*	*Height (inches)*	
BORAGE *Borago officinalis*	Fresh leaves; also flowers	Sow seeds in early spring	¼ inch fine soil	1 foot	Fast	Sky blue	18 to 24	Annual
BURNET *Poterium sanguisorba*	Fresh leaves	Best to sow every year in early spring	¼ inch	15 inches	Slow	Bronze-red	Keep cut to 5 or 6 inches	Perennial
CALAMUS *Acorus calamus*	Flower, foliage, and roots	Plant rhizomes or plants in autumn		1 foot		Purplish blue	36 to 60	Perennial
CAMOMILE *Anthemis nobilis*	Flower heads; fresh leaves	Sow seeds or set plants in April or September	¼ inch	6 inches	Slow	Yellow centre with white rays	15	Perennial
CARAWAY *Carum carvi*	Leaves and roots—fresh; seeds—dried	Sow seeds April	¼ inch	8 to 12 inches	Slow	White	12 to 24	Annual or Biennial
CATNIP *Nepeta cataria*	Fresh or dried	Sow seeds or set plants in spring or fall	¼ inch	6 to 8 inches	Slow	White	18 to 36	Perennial
CHERVIL *Anthriscus cerefolium*	Fresh or dried	Sow seeds in spring or autumn preferably autumn	¼ inch	6 to 8 inches	Slow	White	18 to 21	Annual

NAME	FORM USED	CULTIVATION—GROWTH—HABITS						TYPE OF PLANT
		When to plant	*Depth to sow seed*	*Spacing of plants*	*Germination time*	*Colour of blossom*	*Height (inches)*	
CHICORY *Cichorium intybus*	Flowers for colourful back-grounds; roots	Sow seed from March to May and September	¼ inch	8 to 12 inches	Slow	Bright blue	12 to 36	Perennial
CHIVES *Allium schoenoprasum*	Fresh tops (leaves) Keep cut before flowering	Set bulblets spring or autumn	Set bulblets about 3 inches deep	5 inches	Slow	Lavender	6 to 8	Perennial
CLARY *Salvia sclarea*	Fresh flowers and leaves	Sow seeds in early spring	¼ inch	18 inches	Slow	White or lilac	24	Annual
COMMON SPEEDWELL *Veronia officinalis*	Ornamental flowers and seeds	Sow seeds or set plants in spring	¼ inch	6 to 8 inches	Slow	Pale blue	3 to 10	Perennial
CORAINDER *Coriandrum sativum*	Seeds dried	Sow seeds in spring or autumn	¼ inch	8 to 12 inches	Slow	Whitish	24 to 30	Annual
COSTMARY *Chrysanthemum balsamita*	Fresh leaves	Set plants early spring		10 to 12 inches		Yellow	36 to 48	Perennial
CRESSES UPLAND *Barbarea verna*	Fresh leaves	Early spring			About 50 days			Perennial

HERB GROWING CHART

NAME	FORM USED	CULTIVATION—GROWTH—HABITS						TYPE OF PLANT
		When to plant	*Depth to sow seed*	*Spacing of plants*	*Germination time*	*Colour of blossom*	*Height (inches)*	
CRESSES WATER *Nasturtium officinalis*	Fresh leaves	Early spring Start seeds in pots; transplant to streams	$\frac{1}{8}$ inch		Fast		$2\frac{1}{2}$	Perennial
GARDEN *Lepidium sativum*	Fresh leaves	Early spring Stream not necessary, but keep well watered	$\frac{1}{8}$ inch		Fast		$2\frac{1}{2}$	Annual
CUMIN *Cuminum cyminum*	Seeds	Sow seeds in spring	$\frac{1}{4}$ inch	8 to 10 inches	Slow	Lilac	6	Annual
DANDELION *Taraxacum officinale*	Young leaves; fresh blooms	Sow seeds in March or April	$\frac{1}{4}$ inch	1 to 2 feet	Fast	Yellow	12 to 18	Perennial
DILL *Anethum graveolens*	Green branches; fresh seeds; dried seeds	Sow seeds or set plants in early spring	$\frac{1}{4}$ inch fine soil	1 foot	Medium	Yellow	24 to 36	Annual
FENNELS *Foeniculum*	Fresh stalks; fresh leaves; dried leaves	May or June	$\frac{1}{4}$ inch	18 inches	Reasonably fast	Yellow	24 to 48	Annual

CULTIVATION—GROWTH—HABITS

NAME	FORM USED	When to plant	Depth to sow seed	Spacing of plants	Germination time	Colour of blossom	Height (inches)	TYPE OF PLANT
FENNEL FLOWER *Nigella sativa*	Dried seeds	Sow seed in spring	¼ inch	12 to 18 inches	Slow	Greyish-blue	Small low branches	Annual
FEVERFEW *Chrysanthemum parthenium*	Flowers for background planting and arrangements	Early spring root division		12 to 18 inches		White	24	Perennial
GARLIC *Allium sativum*	Cloves or dried sets	Set bulblets early spring or seed in August –September	Set each bulb separately	4 to 6 inches	Seeds slow Likes shade and moisture	White	6	Perennial
GERANIUMS								
ROSE *Pelargonium graveolens*	Green leaves for flavour and fragrance	Set plants in spring or cuttings in August		18 to 24 inches		Lavender-pink	24	Perennial— treat as Annual
LEMON *Pelargonium limonseum*	Green leaves for flavour and fragrance	Set plants in spring or cutting in August		12 to 14 inches			24	Perennial— treat as Annual
GERMANDER *Teucrium chamaedrys*	Fresh leaves	Sow seeds or set plants in early spring	¼ inch	Good edging plant; 12 inches	Fast	Rosy	6 to 12	Perennial
HOP *Humulus lupulus*	Fresh seed; pods and dried pods	Sow seeds in spring	½ inch	12 to 18 inches	Medium	Yellow	4 to 8 feet	Perennial

HERB GROWING CHART

		CULTIVATION—GROWTH—HABITS						
NAME	FORM USED	When to plant	Depth to sow seed	Spacing of plants	Germina-tion time	Colour of blossom	Height (inches)	TYPE OF PLANT
HOREHOUND *Marrubium vulgare*	Fresh leaves and flowering tops	Sow seed in early spring	¼ inch	12 to 15 inches	Slow	White	12 to 24	Perennial
HORSE-RADISH *Armoracia rusticana*	Fresh roots	Plant roots or seeds in early spring or autumn	Cover top of roots with 2 inch soil. Seeds ½ inch deep	15 to 18 inches	Slow	White	24 to 36	Perennial
HYSSOP *Hyssopus officinalis*	Fresh or dried leaves and stalks for flavour	Sow seed early spring or get seedlings from herb grower	¼ inch	6 inches	Slow	Blue, pink, or white	24	Perennial
LAVENDER *Lavandula spica*	Fresh or dried leaves and flowers for fragrance	Sow seeds early spring	⅛ to ¼ inches	8 inches	14 to 18 days	Lavender	24 to 36	Perennial
LEEK *Allium porrum*	Fresh leaves and bulbs for flavour—very ornamental flower and leaf	Start seeds in specially pre-pared bed in early spring Plant out in summer	Cover with ¼ inch fine soil	4 to 6 inches	Fast	Lavender, white	30 to 36	Perennial

NAME	FORM USED	CULTIVATION—GROWTH—HABITS						TYPE OF PLANT
		When to plant	Depth to sow seed	Spacing of plants	Germination time	Colour of blossom	Height (inches)	
LEMON VERBENA *Lippia citriodora*	Fresh leaves for fragrance and flavour	Start new plants from seedlings in early spring. Plant in summer		Good mature plants 2 feet		Light lavender	6 to 8 feet	Perennial
LOVAGE *Levisticum officinale*	Stalks and stems fresh; leaves and seeds; rhizome	Sow seeds in late summer	¼ inch	3 to 4 feet	Slow	Yellowish green	5 to 7 feet	Perennial
MARIGOLD, POT *Calendula officinalis*	Buds and pods	Sow seeds in early spring or get plants from herb grower	¼ inch	8 to 10 inches	Slow	Yellow-orange	12 to 18	Annual
MARJORAMS POT MARJORAM *Origanum vulgaris*	Fresh flower buds	Sow seeds in March to April	¼ inch	10 inches	Slow	Pinkish white	24	Perennial
SWEET MARJORAM *Marjorana hortensis*	Fresh or dried leaves	Sow seeds in early spring	¼ inch	8 to 12 inches	70 days	Off-white	10 to 24	Annual
MAY APPLE *Podophyllum peltatum*	Ripe fruit; foliage for ornamental effect	Get plants from herb grower or woodsides		6 to 8 inches		White	12 to 18	Perennial

HERB GROWING CHART

NAME	FORM USED	CULTIVATION—GROWTH—HABITS						TYPE OF PLANT
		When to plant	*Depth to sow seed*	*Spacing of plants*	*Germination time*	*Colour of blossom*	*Height (inches)*	
MINTS								
APPLE MINT *Mentha rotundifolia*	Fresh leaves	Best to get plants from herb grower		Best to grow in beds		Lilac	18 to 36	Perennial
PEPPERMINT *Mentha piperita*	Fresh leaves and stalks	Best to get plants from herb grower		6 to 8 inches		Reddish-violet	24	Perennial
SPEARMINT *Mentha spicata*	Fresh for flavour; dried for arrangements	Early spring or autumn		Best to grow in moist soil		Pinkish-lavender	10 to 14	Perennial
MUSTARD								
BLACK *Sinapis nigra*	Leaves—fresh; seeds—dried	Sow seeds in early spring	¼ inch	12 inches	Fast	Yellow	18 inches	Annual
WHITE *Sinapis alba*	Leaves—fresh; seeds—dried	Sow seeds in early spring	¼ inch	12 inches	Fast	Yellow	18 inches	Annual
NASTURTIUM *Tropaeolum minus*	Leaves and flowers—fresh; seeds—green	Sow seeds in early spring	1 inch	6 to 8 inches	Fast	Yellow, orange to dark red	1 to 8	Annual or Biennial
Tropaeolum majus (Indian Cress)	Leaves and …	Sow seeds in April	1 inch	12 inches	Fast	Yellow, orange…	5 to 10 feet	Annual

CULTIVATION—GROWTH—HABITS

NAME	FORM USED	When to plant	Depth to sow seed	Spacing of plants	Germina-tion time	Colour of blossom	Height (inches)	TYPE OF PLANT
ORÉGANO *Origanum vulgare virens*	Leaves—fresh or dried	Best to get plants from herb grower		12 to 15 inches		Lavender	18 to 24	Perennial
PARSLEY *Petroselinum crispum*	Fresh leaves	Sow seeds in spring or autumn	⅛ inch	Good border plant	Slow		6 to 8	Annual or Biennial
PENNYROYAL *Mentha pulegium*	Leaves—fresh or dried	Set plants early spring		5 to 6 inches		Lilac-blue	10 to 12	Perennial
PEPPERS PEPPER TABASCO *Capsicum frutescens*	Crushed or powdered	Best to get plants from herb grower		12 inches		Red pods	18	Annual
SMALL RED CHILI PEPPERS	Mexican chili pods, crushed or powdered	Best to get plants from herb grower		12 inches		Bright red pods	18	Annual
POPPY *Papaver somniferum*	Flowers for border; seeds for flavour	Sow seeds in spring	¼ inch sifted soil	8 to 10 inches	Slow	White to light blue	24 to 36	Annual
RHUBARB *Rheum rhaponticum*	Stalk and leaf for arrangements; stalk fresh for flavour	Roots from herb grower spring and autumn		12 to 15 inches		Yellow	10 to 12	Perennial

HERB GROWING CHART

NAME	FORM USED	CULTIVATION—GROWTH—HABITS						TYPE OF PLANT
		When to plant	Depth to sow seed	Spacing of plants	Germination time	Colour of blossom	Height (inches)	
ROCAMBOLE *Allium scorodoprasum*	Seeds or cloves; later—the new growth leaves	Plant sets in early spring	Cover with 1 inch of soil	6 to 8 inches		Rose-coloured	36	Perennial
ROSEMARY *Rosmarinus officinalis*	Fresh leaves	Sow seeds in early spring	¼ inch	18 inches	Fast	Pale blue	24 to 36	Perennial
ROSES DAMASK *Rosa damascena*	Bushes for ornamental effect; petals for flavour and fragrance	Spring or autumn		2 feet or more		Pink or cream	2 to 5 feet	Perennial
PROVENCE *Rosa gallica*	Petals for flavour and fragrance	Spring or autumn		2 feet or more		Red	3 to 5 feet	Perennial
EGLANTINE *Rosa eglanteria*	Petals for flavour and fragrance	Spring or autumn		2 feet or more		Pink	3 to 5 feet	Perennial
RUE *Ruta graveolens*	Ornamental shrub—fresh and dried	Sow in spring	¼ inch	18 inches	Slow	Greenish-yellow	18 to 24	Perennial
SAGE *Salvia officinalis*	Fresh or dried leaves	Plants from herb grower		6 to 8 inches		Violet-blue	18 to 24	Perennial
SANTOLINAS *S. chamaecyparissus; S. virens*	Fresh and dried leaves; lovely for use in arrangements	Plants from herb grower		3 feet		Yellow	Lavender Cotton, 18 Emerald Green, 24	Perennial

HERB GROWING CHART

NAME	FORM USED	CULTIVATION—GROWTH—HABITS						TYPE OF PLANT
		When to plant	*Depth to sow seed*	*Spacing of plants*	*Germination time*	*Colour of blossom*	*Height (inches)*	
SAVORY								
SUMMER *Satureia hortensis*	Fresh and dried	Sow seeds in early spring	¼ inch	6 to 8 inches	Medium	Dainty pink	12 to 18	Annual
WINTER *Satureia montana*	Fresh or dried leaves	Root division in September and early spring; sow seed in early spring		10 to 12 inches	Slow	White or purplish	15 to 18	Perennial
SESAME *Sesamum orientale*	Ornamental effect; dried seeds for flavour; fresh leaves for teas	Sow seeds in spring	¼ inch	8 inches		Pink-lavender		Annual
SHALLOT *Allium ascalonicum*	Fresh or dried bulb	Set bulbs in spring and autumn		16 inches		Seldom flower	8 to 10	Perennial
SORREL								
FRENCH *R. scutatus*	Fresh leaves	Sow seeds or set bulbs Early spring		1 foot	About 60 days		3 to 4	Perennial
GARDEN *R. acetosa*	Fresh leaves	Bulblets in spring		6 to 9 inches		Pinkish lavender or		
WOOD *Oxalis violacea*	Beauty of leaf and blossom	Plant bulbs in spring		6 to 9 inches		magenta	4 to 9	Perennial

HERB·GROWING CHART

NAME	FORM USED	CULTIVATION—GROWTH—HABITS						TYPE OF PLANT
		When to plant	*Depth to sow seed*	*Spacing of plants*	*Germination time*	*Colour of blossom*	*Height (inches)*	
SWEET BASIL *Ocimum basilicum*	Fresh or dried leaves for flavour	Sow seeds in early spring; transplant when 3″ tall	⅛ to ¼ inch fine soil	12 inches (seedling)	Slow	Pink	12 to 24	Annual
SWEET CICELY *Myrrhis odorata*	Ornamental or fresh leaves for flavour	Sow seeds in autumn or roots in the spring	¼ inch	18 inches	Very slow	White	24	Perennial
SWEET WOODRUFF *Asperula odorata*	Fresh flowers for arrangements; fresh leaves for fragrance and flavour	Best to get plants from herb grower		6 inches		White	1 to 2 (low growing ground cover)	Perennial
TANSY *Tanacetum vulgare*	Fresh or dried for flower arrangements; fresh foliage	Early spring; best from root division		For border or 2 to 3 feet		Yellow	36	Perennial
TARRAGON *Artemisia dracunculus*	Fresh or dried leaves	Best to get plants from herb grower		18 inches		White		Perennial

HERB GROWING CHART

NAME	FORM USED	CULTIVATION—GROWTH—HABITS						TYPE OF PLANT
		When to plant	*Depth to sow seed*	*Spacing of plants*	*Germination time*	*Colour of blossom*	*Height (inches)*	
THYME *Thymus vulgaris*	Leaves and stems	Sow seeds when weather is thoroughly settled	Barely covered with sifted soil	12 inches	Slow	Lavender	12 to 18	Perennial
WILD GINGER *Asarum canadense*	Foliage for ornamental effect; roots for flavour	Spring		8 to 10 inches		Reddish-brown	8 to 10	Perennial
WINTERGREEN *Gaultheria procumbens*	Fresh leaves; ripe berries	Spring		Set in beds or patches		White	2 to 6	Perennial
YARROW *Achillea millefolium*	Flower stalks for arrangements; leaves for teas	Best to get plants from herb grower		10 to 12 inches		White or pink	24 to 36	Perennial

SUGGESTED PATTERNS FOR GROWING

MODEL PERENNIAL HERB GARDEN

Supplies a family of six or more with plenty of fresh herbs for summer use, as well as dried herbs for winter use.

Rear of garden—north or west. Building, fence, or hedge should be here.

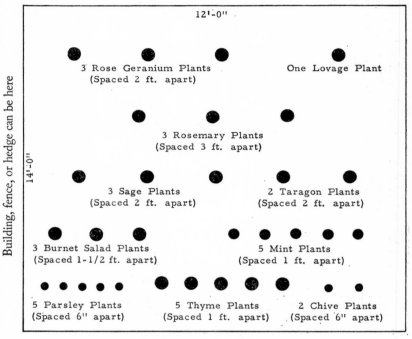

South or east should be open

Furnished through the courtesy of Farmer Seed and Nursery Company, Faribault, Minnesota.

PERENNIAL HERB GARDEN COLLECTION

3 Burnet Salad Plants	2 Clumps Chives	3 Rose Geranium Plants
1 Lovage Plant	5 Parsley Plants	5 Thyme Plants
3 Sage Plants	2 Tarragon Plants	3 Rosemary Plants
	5 Mint Plants	

MODEL ANNUAL HERB GARDEN

To supply the average family

Rear of garden—north or west. Building, fence, or hedge should be here.

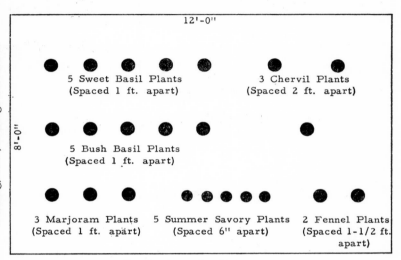

South or east should be open

*Furnished through the courtesy of Farmer Seed and Nursery Company,
Faribault, Minnesota.*

ANNUAL HERB GARDEN COLLECTION

3 Chervil Plants	3 Marjoram Plants	5 Bush Basil Plants
2 Fennel Plants	5 Summer Savoury Plants	5 Sweet Basil Plants

Courtesy of Breck's of Boston

SMALL HERB GARDEN
(6 feet in diameter)

Can be made from a three terrace garden pyramid.

SMALL HERB GARDEN

Can be made from aluminium grass barrier,
discarded bricks, or solite concrete blocks.

174

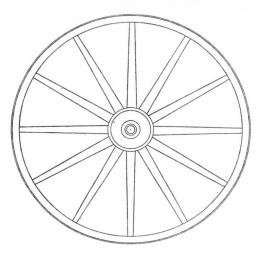

SMALL HERB GARDEN

Can be made from a discarded wagon wheel.

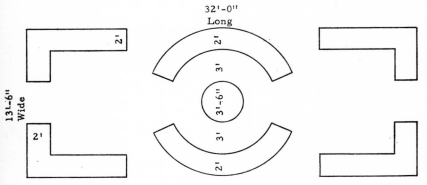

Courtesy of Wayside Gardens, Mentor, Ohio

SEMI-FORMAL 'WAYSIDE' HERB GARDEN

Would be nice bordering driveways.

Herb beauty for terraces and borders·
No. 1.   Low growing herbs for edging borders .
No. 2.   Medium growing herbs for blooms and ornamental foliage.
No. 3.   Tall growing herbs for background planting.
(Please see growing chart.)

HERB BEAUTY FOR TERRACES AND BORDERS

No. 1. Low-growing herbs for edging borders.
No. 2. Medium-growing herbs for blooms and ornamental foliage.
No. 3. Tall-growing herbs for background planting.
(Please see growing chart.)

Brighten garage or garden wall with
herb planted window boxes

A plant or two of rose geranium, sage, or chives taken up from the herb garden and reset in a pot of good soil will do well all winter if kept watered and in a sunny window. Parsley for seasoning can also be kept in this manner. This is one herb whose appearance, fragrance, and flavour are welcome through the drab winter months.

ENLARGED HERB GARDEN

Can be made from aluminium grass barrier,
discarded bricks, or solite concrete blocks

6. Yesterday, today and tomorrow

HINTS FOR PREPARING
AND DRYING HERBS

DRYING: Select choice new growth when it's at the peak of perfection. Cut herbs in the early morning; tie in bunches and hang over a stretched wire in a dark airy room, after sun-drying. While leaves are being dried, spread them thinly on a screen and place screen in dark airy room. Leaves will dry in colour. When herbs are dry place in airtight jars.

When drying herbs, flowers for fragrance, and flowers for winter bouquets, cut just when they come into bloom. Tie in bunches, hang upside down in dark, airy room to dry in colour.

HINTS FOR FREEZING
AND THAWING HERBS

FREEZING: May be packed without blanching. Cut only the finest and nicest leaves and stems, wash carefully under spigot, drain dry in a wire backet. Then dry-pack in plastic bags. Label with cards or foil placed inside bag. Make bag airtight and place in freezer immediately.

THAWING: Keep herbs in their original containers while thawing if possible. Place on table in room, allow thirty to forty minutes to thaw. A watertight package may be thawed in cold running water in twenty minutes. The package should be removed from the water as soon as thawing is complete. For best flavour use immediately. Use like fresh herbs, if possible.

PART TWO

Assembly of the Spices

7. Assembly of the spices

All that mankind has done, thought, gained or been: it is lying in magic preservation in the pages of books.

They are the chosen possessions of men.

THOMAS CARLYLE

Have you ever imagined the magnitude of thought that went into the planning of the very first garden? The Garden of Eden must have been like this:

FIRST, there must have been all the shades of green to rest the eyes . . . and then all the colours of the rainbow to lift the spirits.

SECOND, there must have been fragrance—beautiful, subtle, and inviting.

THIRD, there must have been the tantalizing sight of mouth-watering fruit—sun-ripened peaches and cherries hanging like precious jewels on the boughs—to give exotic flavours.

In the first garden there was made to grow every tree that was beautiful to look upon, . . . bearing an abundance of fruit good to eat. There were clear waters, lilies of the field, and sweet-smelling herbs.

Through the misty curtains of the past we glimpse the earliest spice and herb gatherers, who must truly have been the children of nature: enjoying the songs of birds, the life-giving sunshine, the slopes, the hills, the mountains and all of the floor levels of the earth, the refreshing rains, the streams, the rivers, and the star-studded roof of the heavens.

From Arabia came the camel caravans, whose merchants worked feverishly to load their camels for the long, arduous, and dangerous trek to faraway places with their precious merchandise. Spices were the basis of our earliest trade and commerce. The ancients sold ointments and oils for very large sums of money to the wealthy ruling classes, who wanted soothing balms and sweet fragrances to fill their homes. The first gifts of the Wise Men were frankincense from the East African *Boswellia* tree; myrrh from the Arabian and East African *Balsamodendron myrrha* shrub; and other sweet-smelling herbs brought in vases and cups made from the ornamental murra stone from ancient Rome.

Romantic associations are attached to many of our spices. The bay tree (*Laurus nobilis*), Dr John Lindley tells us, is sometimes called Apollo's laurel. In *Chambers's Cyclopaedia of English Literature* (1853) Warton tells a romantic little story that is truly a treasure:

> *The daughter of the king of Hungary having fallen into melancholy, in consequence of the loss of her lover, the squire of low degree, her father thus endeavours to console her. The passage is valuable, 'because'*, says Warton, *'it delineates in lively colours, the fashionable diversions and usages of ancient times.'*

Extract from *The Squire of Low Degree:*

Tomorrow ye shall in hunting fare
Be seated in a velvet chair—
Ye shall have harp and song
And other mirths among.
Ye shall have Rumney and Malespine
And other Vernage wine [a drink made of wine, honey, and spices]
When ye are laid in a bed so soft,
A cage of gold will be hung aloft—
With long paper fair burning
And cloves that be sweet smelling.
Frankincense and olibanum
That where ye sleep the taste will come—
And if ye no rest can take,
All night minstrels for ye shall wake.

The clove tree is another treasure that should be dear to all of us because of its fragrance and flavour. Gerard has said, 'Tho this description be very brief—it has none that can compare—their smell is so pleasing it is like the pepper-nut more fragile—it is grown in the Indian ground but was brought to us from the Eastern Spice Islands for the smell.'

The island of Zanzibar, just off the east coast of Africa, used to be noted as a centre of the slave trade but since this is now a thing of the past its great claim to fame is cloves. Its symmetrical, shiny green, and red-stemmed clove trees are second only to those of the Far Eastern Spice Islands. The spicy stimulating odour permeates the island. Dr David Livingstone started from Zanzibar to try to find the Mountain of the Moon. His body is buried in England but his heart was laid away in the African wilderness. It was here that he cried out in a resounding voice against the slave trade.

The ancients spoke eloquently of the cinnamon tree. They described its beautiful leaves, and how the bark, when taken off and cast on the ground in the heat of the sun, gave off a warm sweetness of smell. They also mentioned the nutmeg tree, which makes a goodly show when well laden with fruit. They pointed out that nutmeg would sweeten the breath if held in the mouth and much chewed upon.

Most spices, at least the earliest known ones, were indigenous to China. They were taken into India by camel caravans over back-breaking land routes that varied in level from the lowest steppe to the highest mountain. From India they were taken to Arabia and Egypt. Not until the Crusades brought East and West face to face in the Holy Land did European appetites quicken at the pungent Eastern flavours. To satisfy this new European desire and demand for these exotic flavours from the East, ships began plying the Mediterranean, carrying spices to the large metropolitan seaports along the southern coast of Europe. It was natural that Venice, with its cosmopolitan tastes and huge shipping interests, should control this trade. Venice maintained a monopoly on spice shipping until Portugal found new sea routes to the East.

These new routes were found because of the constant battling for control of trade on the seas. Competition brought about more ship-building and created an ever-growing interest among the navigators and explorers of many countries such as Magellan from Portugal and Columbus, the Italian navigator. Most of this trade was in spices!

The next glimpse between the unfurled curtains was of ships sailing down through the next hundred and fifty years, their explorers and navigators searching their charts and setting their courses for the unknown. Literally they searched each wave for a clue to the lands beyond the horizons. In looking for new sea routes to the East, Columbus discovered America.

The drama for which the stage was set by Columbus is portrayed in some verses written in the eighteenth century by George Berkeley, a bishop to whom the Pope assigned 'every virtue under Heaven'.

The Muse, disgusted at an age and clime
*   Barren of every glorious theme,*
In distant times now waits a better time,
*   Producing subjects worthy fame.*

In happy climes, where from the genial sun
*   An virgin earth, such scenes ensue,*
The force of art by nature seems outdone,
*   And fancied beauties by the true:*

In happy climes, the seat of innocence,
*   Where nature guides and virtue rules.*
Where men shall not impose for truth and sense
*   The pedantry of courts and schools:*

There shall be sung another golden age,
*   The rise of empire and of arts,*
The good and great inspiring epic rage,
*   The wisest heads and noblest hearts.*

Not such as Europe breeds in her decay;
*   Such as she bred when fresh and young,*
When heavenly flame did animate her clay
*   By future poets shall be sung.*

Westward the course of empire takes its way;
*   The four first acts already past,*
A fifth shall close the drama with the day;
*   Time's noblest offspring is the last.*

The early use of spices and herbs is most intriguing, but one side of the spice picture seems to have escaped many of us. While we tend to think only in terms of flavourings and seasonings, history and legend tell of many other uses in medieval times. These included the preserving of food and the preparation of dyes, perfumes, medicines, and confections.

In our modern use of scintillating spices and herbs we are becoming more aware of our priceless heritage of fragrance and flavour. It is hoped that the story unfolded on the previous pages will inspire others to become more aware of the wondrous beauty, exciting fragrance, and exotic flavours that surround us in all phases of the commercial world of today. For spices and fragrant perfumes, we go to the merchants, but for the unlimited varieties of herbs, we should go to the seedsman, the nurseryman, and the garden shop where these lovely gifts of nature can be obtained. By growing them in our gardens we can add excitement and enjoyment to our everyday living.

8. Stories of the spices

PEPPER
Piper nigrum

The spiciest of all spices—that's pepper. It is the most important and authoritative of all. We know it carries itself with great authority because it asserts itself immediately when we bring it too close to our nostrils. As a seasoning it is second only to salt, its twin. It is on practically every table in the world and is used at every meal. Pepper makes almost everything taste better.

Nothing has had a more romantic history than pepper. The pepper shrub originally came from the Malabar district on the west coast of India, but today eighty per cent of the pepper supply comes from the old Dutch Indies. Sarawak, in the northern part of Borneo, is one of the chief producers, and Chinese farmers grow most of Sarawak's pepper. Apparently the Chinese first came to this area more than a thousand years ago to work in the rice fields, but the rice crop proved to be unprofitable. Those who did not turn to trade became rubber or pepper growers. Their pepper gardens average only about five acres, for the British discouraged large estates.

The Greeks were using pepper as early as the fourth century B.C., but in ancient and medieval times only the rich could afford it. It came from the Far East by caravan, and to reach Europe it had to be transported halfway around the world over the most tortuous routes imaginable. The expense was so great that a pound of pepper was considered to be 'fit for a king'.

It seems that pepper is one of two things that people all around the world have had to have. Unlike salt, it is not essential to life itself, but it is certainly essential to a good disposition. Since it is so important, it was quite natural that pepper should have been used as money. Taxes and tribute have been paid with pepper. When Alaric the Goth besieged Rome, the ransom demanded from the city was five thousand pounds of gold, thirty thousand pounds of silver, and three thousand pounds of pepper. The Romans had the gold and the silver, but they had a very difficult time getting together the pepper portion of the ransom. Toward the end of the tenth century English landlords charged a rent tax of one pound of pepper a year. It was a valuable part of the spoils obtained by victorious soldiers. The very high price set on pepper was one of the reasons Portugal sought (and found) a water route to India. The cost of pepper in Europe dropped tremendously when the way was found around the Cape of Good Hope.

Here is what Gerard says about pepper in his great *Herball:* 'The Plant that beareth the blacke pepper groweth up like a vine, amongst bushes and brambles, where it naturally groweth but where it is manured it is fowne at the bottom of tree Janfel and the Date tree, whereon it taketh hold and clymbeth up even unto the top, as doth the vine, ramping and taking hold with his clasping tendrels of any other thing. All pepper heateth, provoketh, digesteth, draweth, disperseth, and clenseth the dimness of the sight, as Dioscorides noteth.'

Pepper comes from the fruit or seeds of a climbing shrub that will grow wild. However, most of it is cultivated on plantations where shrubs are grown from seeds or cuttings. The shrub yields fruit in three years and reaches top yield in seven years. Black pepper is made by drying unripe berries until they are black. White pepper is made by grinding only the seeds taken from the berry.

Black pepper is much stronger than white pepper. The next time you pass a container of black pepper, shake some out on your hand and you will notice that there are white grains mixed with the black grains. Most black pepper is marketed for home use as a mixture. White pepper is used to buffer, or tone down, the piercing flavour of pure black pepper.

To get the most enjoyment out of pepper, use a grinder and grind the berries fresh for every meal. Its fragrance and flavour, just after grinding, will give you a new taste thrill.

A quaint 'Item for Housekeepers' (in a Manchester, New Hampshire, newspaper, 1866) says: 'Scatter ground black pepper over your furs and flannels when you lay them away for the summer and the moths will never trouble them.'

So that's pepper, a part of our way of life.

On page 136 are two recipes using pepper. It is hoped that you will try both of them. If you can try only one, however, do not miss the experience of tasting Black-Seeded Simpson Salad.

CLOVES
Caryophyllus aromaticus

Everywhere there was an indescribably piquant, pungent, and sweet fragrance, saturating every breath of moisture-laden air rising above the waves of the blue-green sea. As the ship sailed with the breeze, sailors knew they were getting close to the isle of Amboina, thirty miles long and only half as wide. Everywhere on the isle are tiny brilliant blossoms, poised like precious jewels in a dense setting of deep, rich green. It was from here that the sweet fragrance borne on the land breeze let the sailors know they had arrived at the 'Garden of Spices'.

By all size comparisons, the isle of Amboina is small. The romantic history of this small isle would fill several books, some pleasing and some not so pleasing. In the search for 'bouquet' (fragrance and flavour) lives were lost, hardships overcome, wars fought, and even the survival of nations hung on a handful of spice. Great wealth was gained and lost but lasting satisfaction became a part of living because of the acquisition of this *bouquet de piquancy*.

The bouquet was desperately needed by many countries, among

which was medieval England, whose winter diet consisted of coarse meal and salted meat, as cold storage was unknown. Before the winter was over, much of this bare mealtime fare was half spoiled. To cut down on the spoilage and make the food more palatable, those with money were quite willing to pay fantastic sums for small amounts of cloves (along with other members of the 'Big Four'—pepper, cinnamon, and nutmeg). They were worth more than their weight in gold. As a result, even the smallest nations, with no natural sources of great wealth, became rich and powerful beyond belief simply by controlling the spice trade. Portugal, the Netherlands, and England did so and are still reaping benefits because the spices have remained invaluable, even in these 'deepfreezer' days!

Now another look at Amboina, which with a few close-by smaller islands makes up the 'clove garden'. Amboina is one of the true spice islands, one of the Moluccas, which are in turn a part of the great Australasian island group. The Moluccas are located east of the Celebes and separate them from New Guinea. Amboina was the first and only home of the rare spicy delicacy, the clove, until it was finally transplanted to Zanzibar and the West Indies. Although it has been witness to many a bloody battle in the past, Amboina is now a quiet, methodical Dutch town, where English traders are welcome, and it is still the centre of the clove world.

A little more about the clove tree. It has been said that nutmegs have to smell the sea and the clove has to see it, to grow to maturity properly. This saying has been borne out through centuries as the clove tree prospered in salt air. It is truly a magnificent tree, an evergreen that sometimes grows to a height of forty feet and blooms the whole year round. The flower buds are a pale colour at first; they turn gradually to green and then to bright red. At this stage they are ready for picking. Drying to a dark brown hue prevents them from decaying. They then shrivel to the brownish-black and spicy titbits we know as cloves. They are about half an inch long and the knob of one end contains unopened flower petals in the form of a ball. The clove looks like a nail and because of this it was given its name from the French word *clou*, meaning nail.

In addition to their very widespread use in our food, cloves have always occupied an important place in the 'world of perfumery'. The oils extracted from the clove are indeed precious to the scent maker. Cloves have also found themselves in demand by the 'concocter of confections', and the field of medicine has utilized them here and there in many varied ways. The best-known use of cloves in medicine is as a soother for toothache. For this, oil of clove is used. The oil is obtained by repeated distillation in water.

The flowers of the clove tree, which grows only in the East and West Indies, were first used for decoration. They were used by ancient China in 266 B.C., when the emperor ordered his courtiers to hold cloves in their mouths while in his presence. Cloves were used by Romans, Greeks, and Persians as a base in many of their love philters.

To have the scent of cloves in our own gardens, we can grow clove pinks and clove gillyflowers. The Arabs of North Africa, more than two thousand years ago, used the petals of spicy pinks to give a pleasing taste to the bitter herb tonics they used to abate fever. Pinks were also used as a medium of exchange when the Arabs crossed the Mediterranean to Spain. A different species of pinks was used by early Romans in the chaplets they wore at banquets.

CINNAMON
Cinnamomum
zeylanicum
of the laurel family

In a far-off place man found a tree that now has the botanical name of *Cinnamomum zeylanicum*. It is a native to the Far East, particularly to Ceylon and India. The tree is unusual in that it has a double bark . . . and from the inner bark comes the distinctive and distinguished 'bouquet' we know as cinnamon

It has been used since biblical times, first in combination with myrrh and aloes as a body scent or perfume (Proverbs 7:17); it was also burned in the temples of the gods as an incense.

It is believed that Galle, the oldest Ceylon seaport, was the Tarshish of the Bible and belonged to the Phoenician traders. Here it might have been that King Solomon obtained his pearls and other riches.

Ceylon has been the cinnamon capital of the world from biblical times until today. Cinnamon was the deadly lure of Ceylon's European conquerors. First came the Portuguese in 1505; they monopolized the cinnamon trade until 1658, when the Dutch decided to take over. The Dutch had a magnificent reign until 1796 when the English found that they were missing out on a very profitable trade. They wrested control from the Dutch and managed to hold on until 1948, when Ceylon was granted dominion status.

Incidentally, the British, when they first took over the island, were able to do what neither the Portuguese nor the Dutch could accomplish—they liquidated the kingdom of Kandy high up in the mountains. As an aid, they used a weapon of 'psychological warfare'; the devout Singhalese believed that whoever held Buddha's sacred tooth was the island's rightful ruler, so the British captured the tooth and brought the whole kingdom under their control.

When the enterprising Dutch were in control, the penalty for the illegal sale of even a single stick of cinnamon was death. This penalty remained in effect until the Dutch gave in to the English. The control of the spice trade was of such importance that England formed the East India Company to undermine the Dutch. This company was all-powerful. It had trading centres in all important seaports of the world, including Boston, then the hub of the Massachusetts Colony, Britain's newly found source of wealth in America. By operating as one huge unit, the East India Company was able to exert its influence all over the globe, applying a little pressure here and there and making uncomfortable situations for its competitors.

As one leaves Colombo, Ceylon's capital, it is necessary to pass through the 'City of Gardens', a beautiful collection and a summary of the world's best in fragrance and flavour. These gardens are intended to be a reminder that for many centuries the spice trade, and especially cinnamon, was Ceylon's greatest source of wealth.

Cinnamon is another 'island plant', like cloves and nutmeg. It does best near the ocean with its salty breezes. It is a spice from the true spice islands and sailors, when near the islands, always know where they are by the fragrance wafting outward to them.

The cinnamon tree is a beautiful thing. It is an evergreen with gorgeous leaves, not unlike the orange tree, but it has the deep dark green colour of the bay tree. The flowers are a white delight and they turn into sparkling round berries that resemble those of a ripe olive tree. When the berries are chafed between the hands a fragrance that cannot be adequately described fills the air. Trying to imagine this fragrance without experiencing it is like learning a song without singing it. Like the cork tree, the trunk or woody body is covered with double bark. When the whole bark is stripped from the tree and the inner bark is placed on the ground under the hot sun, it curls and folds into itself and looks like a roll of wrapping paper. Experience has shown that it is at its best when it has dried to a light brown colour. Every three years the ritual of debarking the cinnamon tree is carried out and with great pleasure, because it means that money or some medium of exchange will be forthcoming. Cinnamon deserves its seat of honour in every spice cabinet.

From the English the early American colonists learned the use of cinnamon in their 'winter warmers'. These were hot drinks made from rum, boiling water, spices, butter, and cinnamon sticks. They were served in tankards or mugs, always before an open fire.

NUTMEG
AND MACE
*Myristica
moschata*

Here is a 'companion pair'—brothers under the skin that come from a paradisaical setting to find their way into many of our culinary delights. There must be nutmeg trees in Paradise because they pass the entrance requirements for beauty and bounty.

Of the more than eighty species of nutmeg trees and shrubs, the most common is a luxuriant evergreen with branches from the bottom to the top of its straight trunk—it grows to a height of about twenty-five feet. During the blooming season it is covered with small yellow flowers that generate a fragrance similar to that of lilies of the valley. The tree blooms and bears continuously the year round, yielding a yellow fruit about the size of a pear. The colour harmony is almost matchless, with spots of yellow waving in the wind among broad leaves that are a deep, dark, glossy green on top and lined with silver on the bottom.

The nutmeg tree is another island tree that grows primarily in the Netherlands Indies, the West Indies, and on the island of Penang, which is just off the west coast of the Malay Peninsula. The Banda Islands in the Molucca group are the most famous for the quality of their nutmeg-bearing products.

This tree should be called the nutmeg and mace tree. The reason will be obvious as the harvesting and processing steps are described. The fruit is picked when fully ripe and the outer husk is removed. This husk is the firsy 'goody' obtained from the fruit. It is preserved in syrup and looked upon in the Netherlands Indies as a rare delicacy. Mace, the woven scarlet fruit fibre, is under the outer husk and inside the mace is the musky little nutmeg seed surrounded by its aril. The aril withers away, leaving the nut or nutmeg so well known to commerce. It is normally about one inch long and oval-shaped. The mace and nuts are both dried, first on a fire and then in the sun. The drying period is generally a month. The mace is finely ground on the spot but the nuts are exported whole to retain their flavour. Oil of mace and nutmeg butter are made from nuts of inferior quality, which are ground to extract the oil.

The history of nutmeg and mace is tied to that of the over-all spice trade, which has been described previously. The first mention of nutmeg appeared in the twelfth century when it was described as a street fumigant. It was usually laid in piles and burned when some person of high esteem was expected to visit the city. Not much was known of nutmeg, however, until the sixteenth century, when the Dutch started to exploit the newly found sea route to the Far East, where fragrant and flavoursome riches and treasures lay waiting. When the Dutch ran across the Moluccas they organized them into a tight, closely guarded unit that systematically produced for them. Originally the Banda Islands (part of the Moluccas) were made the sole home of the nutmeg tree so as to restrict its growth and thereby make it more valuable in the field of commerce. The seed-carrying birds, however, did not 'know' about these restrictions!

Several medicinal uses for nutmeg are listed in reference books, among them one described as a cure for insomnia. Very probably the nutmeg, with its unusually different bouquet, simply erased cares and worries from the mind of the insomnia sufferer, thus making it possible to drift quietly off to dreamland.

One of my earliest memories of shopping for my mother concerns nutmeg. She would send me to the store with a nickel to buy three nutmegs that were later grated on a tiny nutmeg grater and used on baked custards, which were served in individual brown custard cups. This brings to mind a quotation:

> Be as rough as a nutmeg grater and rogues will obey you well.
>
> ORAN HILL

So that is nutmeg—it lives in its mace until it is ready to find its place, along with the mace, in your spice cabinet.

NUTMEG . . . with its aromatic pungency!

and MACE . . . with its tender, sweet mildness!

ALLSPICE
Pimenta officinalis
of the myrtle family

Allspice is truly a wondrous creation of nature. The fruit is about the size of a black currant and resembles a peppercorn. So aptly named, it combines the overtones of fragrance and flavour that make cinnamon, cloves, and nutmeg among the jewels of food flavourings. Allspice means exotic bouquet—a bouquet with the full-bodied pleasantness of the clove, the soothing velvet of the nutmeg, and the rich aroma of cinnamon. All of these can be readily found by putting a small amount of ground allspice on your hand and wafting it under your nose. The fragrance of the three is there as though it were a physical mixture.

The allspice tree is a beautiful tropical American evergreen that resembles the clove tree and the nutmeg tree. The berries are picked while still green and then are sun-dried for about one week or until they turn a dark reddish brown. Allspice is known throughout the spice trade as pimento and this should not be confused with pimiento, which is a species of red pepper used as a garnish.

The finding of allspice was part of the history connected with the intriguing story of the discovery, development, and socialization of the West Indies. Allspice is the only major spice grown exclusively in the Western Hemisphere. Today practically all of the world's production comes from Jamaica, but it is also grown in Mexico, Guatemala, Honduras, Brazil, and the Leeward Islands.

For the newcomer to the wonderful experience of seasoning with the spices, there could be no better starting point than allspice.

BAY
Laurus nobilis
of the laurel family

The bay tree is so steeped in history that it is difficult to find its equal. This was the tree most celebrated by ancient poets. Ovid tells with great beauty the fable about Daphne's transformation into a laurel tree to save her from the pursuit of Apollo, who adopted the tree as his own:

> *Because thou canst not be*
> *My mistress, I espouse thee for my tree,*
> *Be thou the prize of honour and renown;*
> *The deathless poet and the poem crown.*
> *Thou shalt the Roman festivals adorn,*
> *And, after poets, be by victors worn.*

OVID

The leaves of the bay tree were considered to be suitable for crowns because of their dedication to the gods of poetry and music. Poets (and they were held in especially high esteem in ancient times) were crowned with 'fashioned' bay leaves. Later the laurel crowns were

197

placed upon the heads of triumphant warriors and victors in the Olympic games. Doctors were also honoured by having the laurel crown placed upon their heads. Poets, warriors, and kings still receive the laurel crown in poetry, on statues, and on coins. In addition, court poets were honoured with the title of laureate.

Besides having a kingly history, the bay tree looks kingly. In southern climates it will exceed thirty feet in height. It is a beautiful evergreen with deep, rich green leaves that are highly but pleasantly aromatic. The bay tree is of the same family as the sassafras and camphor trees, both of which are noted for their aromatic qualities. It does better in the subtropics where the older trees (but only the older ones) bear beautiful yellow flowers and red to black cherry-shaped fruit. The tree is very common throughout the Far East, and there are entire forests of bay trees in the Canary Islands. It can be cultivated, however, in southern Europe and has been completely naturalized in Italy and France. Even in southern England it has been possible to grow one variety successfully, and it is one of England's most beautiful evergreens, thought it will never yield the lovely flowers so common to the tree in the subtropics.

The leaves of the bay tree are laden with a luscious aromatic oil that is much used in medicine as well as cookery. The leaves, when bruised between the fingers, give off a pleasant odour. When burned they give a wonderful, grateful incense. For cooking purposes, bay leaves are used in dried form for both fragrance and flavour.

The husks of the berries contain a great quantity of volatile oil that is very aromatic. Also the kernels, when pressed, furnish an oil that is much used for embrocations. This oil is greenish in colour and faintly resembles in odour that of the bay leaf. Bay rum is the name given to a toilet preparation made by mixing oil of bay with diluted alcohol and adding oil of allspice and oil of orange peel; originally bay rum came from the West Indies. Toilet waters prepared from the one and only bay rum are still used today, and on an ever-widening scale, by discriminating people.

GINGER
Zingiber officinale

Much romantic tradition and history centre about ginger. It has been used since the remotest time and in many different ways. It had several medicinal uses long before it became known as a food 'pepper upper'. Ginger has been chewed as an aid to digestion, to improve the disposition, and to sooth a toothache. Today at least six beverages owe their tantalizing flavour to ginger. A fisherman's tale says that, when ginger is chewed and the juice is applied to the bait, the fish really flock to the hook.

Ginger is a pungent rootstock indigenous to India and China. Today it is grown as an important commercial crop in West Africa, the West Indies, Central America, and Jamaica. It was the first oriental spice to be grown in the New World. In the Middle Ages it was second only to pepper in value, and even as late as the seventeenth century the price of a pound of ginger was the same as the price of a sheep. Marco Polo saw the growing plant and noted this fact in his journal in the year A.D. 1280.

Jamaica ginger is the most valuable of all ginger grown in the world today. It is marketed in two forms: preserved (or green) and dried and cured. Ground ginger (dried and cured) can be obtained in two forms—when the skin is left on the root it is called 'black ginger'; with the skin removed, we have 'white ginger'. The plant usually grows to a height of approximately two feet and the essence of fragrance is to be found in the cured roots and especially in the creamy flowers. Ginger has so fascinated people through the ages that many places and things have ginger associated with their names. One of these is 'The Land of Green Ginger'—the name of a street in Hull, England. It was here that a preserve known as green ginger was made from ginger and lemon juice. It was so delectable to the people of the neighbourhood that they decided to name a street after it.

WILD
GINGER
Asarum canadense

Separate and aside from ginger is wild ginger (*Asarum canadense*). Although it is said to be native to Europe and Asia, the first American colonizers found the Indians growing it. They used wild ginger mainly to make hominy grits, one of their basic foods, more palatable. Wild ginger can be grown in your kitchen herb garden if you can provide deep shade, plenty of water, and rich humus. It is a handsome plant with kidney-shaped leaves and luxuriant, brownish-purple flowers that grow very close to the ground, as though afraid of getting too far away from their natural environment. Of interest is the fact that the flower peeps out of the ground even before the first leaf appears.

Ginseng has often been mistaken for ginger. It is most famous for its medicinal properties, but it has a gingerlike fragrance and flavour and its rootstock is so like that of ginger that it has often been difficult to distinguish them. Similar to both ginger and ginseng is the spikenard plant, best remembered for the 'very precious' ointments made from it during biblical times. Despite their similarity, the spikenard is only a distant relative of ginseng, and ginseng has the same relation to ginger.

Webster must have really known his ginger. His definition says in part that ginger is the spice 'to put life and vigour into'. Its heart-shaped foliage, creamy flowers, and quaint little roots make ginger an important part of our heritage of fragrant beauty.

CARDAMOM
Elettaria
cardamomum
maton
of the Zingiberaceae
family

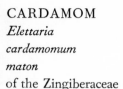

'Grains of Paradise' is a description given to the seeds chewed as a confection by the Arabs in ancient times. The pungent, aromatic cardamom was first used about the eighth century and was a native of India. It is said to have been imported into Europe about the year A.D. 1214.

Gerard's description is fascinating: 'There be divers sorts of Graines, some long, others Peare-fashioned; some greater, and others lesser.' Of the husk, or cod, he says, 'The Cod wherein the hot spice lies, which we call Graines; in shops, Grana Paradisi: it growes, by the report of the Learned, upon a low herby plant; the leaves are some foure inches long, and three broad, with somewhat a thicke middle rib, from which runs transverse fibres, they much in shape resemble those of Cloves. The fruit is like a great cod or huske, in shape like a fig when it groweth upon the tree, but of colour russet, thrust full of small seeds or grains of a darke reddish colour of an exceeding hot taste'. Then Gerard describes the virtues: 'The graines chewed in the mouth draw forth from the head and stomacke waterish and pituitous humors. They also comfort and warm the weake cold and feeble stomack, help the ague, and rid the shaking fits, being drunk with Sacke.'

Cardamom is cultivated today in India, Ceylon, Guatemala, Mexico, Thailand, and Central America. The seeds have a versatile affinity that leads to a broad range of uses from the daintiest dessert to sausage and curry powder.

The Arabs' love of coffee is legend. The brew of Oman and most of Arabia is said to be bitter and black, often flavoured with cardamom, and served in cups like little crucibles.

VANILLA
Vanilla planifolia
of the orchid
family

In the days of Marco Polo sailors talked about the mysterious, enchanted island of Madagascar. They told of a land of dense jungles, towering mountains, and beautiful flowers among which was an exotic, climbing, shimmering golden orchid with oblong and fleshy leaves measuring four inches when mature. The aerial roots and slender stems twine around trees and the flowering branches produce as many as twenty orchids in a cluster. The pods, which contain an abundance of seed, are six to ten inches long and from these pods we obtain vanilla.

The Spanish explorer Cortez was astonished to see the great Aztec ruler Montezuma drink a beverage of chocolate flavoured with vanilla beans. Among all the treasures of Aztec art, gold, and silver returned to Spain, the vanilla beans proved to be no less valuable and appreciated for their delectable flavour. Just enough of them reached Europe to suggest their worthiness but it was many years before the mystery of this temperamental plant was unravelled. A membrane separates the stamen from the pistil so that it cannot fertilize itself. As a result, only one flower in more than a hundred ever matures into a pod under natural conditions. The wind or rare visits of insects were its only sources of pollination until the nineteenth century. About 1835, orchid growers in Madagascar were taught to transfer pollen by hand.

It was here that bean 'rustling' became a problem. Just before harvest time the rustlers would raid the vines. The growers had to start branding the beans just as cattle are branded. The brands were made by using cork and sharp pins to make distinctive patterns that left permanent scars on the green beans.

The beans are harvested about seven months after pollination and then carefully cured, for they are tasteless and odourless until the bouquet inherent in the bean is brought out through fermentation, which causes the formation of a volatile oil called *vanillin*. Curing consists of warming the beans in the sun, after which they are put into 'sweat boxes' where fermentation occurs. These two steps are carried out alternately until the optimum amount of oil is formed. To produce the world's most popular flavour for confections, beverages, and food dishes, the vanillin is dissolved in alcohol. Its popularity extends even to the manufacture of perfumes.

A little town called Antalaha in Madagascar is the capital of the world's production of vanilla beans. Next in line are Mexico and the Netherlands Indies. They are cultivated on a minor scale in Central America, the West Indies, and Tahiti.

TURMERIC
Curcuma longa
of the ginger family

Turmeric is one of the ancient spices that were well known in biblical days. It was used then as a perfume as well as a spice and has always been an important part of the fabulous spice trade. It is native to Indonesia and China, but today India, Haiti, Jamaica, and Peru grow it as an important crop and export quantities to the United States. India has under cultivation vast fields of turmeric with eye-catching fragrant flowers that have pinkish tops and cool yellow blossoms in the middle, and India is the source of most of Britain's supplies. The leaves and stems are a deep rich green. Just as in the case of ginger, turmeric is grown for the roots, which grow to the same size but are far sweeter, more delicate, and have greater fragrance than ginger. The roots of turmeric have a clean, fresh, distinctive aroma. They can be purchased either in whole root form or powdered.

Tumeric lends itself nicely to combination with other spices. It is one of the chief ingredients of curry powder, which has been called the 'salt of the Orient'. Many people prefer turmeric to saffron as a food colouring. This lovely spice is used to impart the appealing colour and mouth-watering delicate taste to mustard sauce and powdered mustard.

Turmeric is one of the more versatile spices. Not only is it used in perfumery, flavouring, and seasoning, it has a place in the huge chemical industry where it is used in a test to detect the presence of alkalis. The natives of India and China use it in dyeing.

SAFFRON
CROCUS
Crocus sativus
of the crocus family

People of the Mediterranean regions valued the saffron crocus for all its virtues long before the Phoenicians carried it over their trade routes to spreading civilizations. Steeped in romance since Queen Nefertiti's time, the saffron crocus has been dedicated to the sun; it was cultivated in King Solomon's garden; Cleopatra used it in some of her favourite cosmetics; early Egyptians used it in their religious ceremonies; and it has been said that in ancient Ireland a king's mantle was dyed with the crocus.

It is the world's most expensive spice, since seventy-five thousand blossoms are required to produce one pound of saffron powder. Because it has always been so costly, the temptation to adulterate it has been great. In Nuremberg in the fifteenth century, dishonest dealers were burned at the stake together with their adulterated saffron.

The crocus is apparently responsible for the crocodile's name. It is said that the crocodile was named for the lovely purple crocus because the only sincere tears he ever shed were forced from him by the blissful fragrance of the saffron crocus.

Paracelsus, one of the early famous physicians, used saffron in concocting all of his medicines. It was used as a specific remedy for gout, whose pain and inflammation it had the power to alleviate, and it was used also for rheumatism.

It was prized as a cosmetic and perfume many centuries ago in Babylon, and even today its delicate piquancy is used in perfumery.

The saffron crocus grows in the flowery meadows of Kashmir's 'Happy Valley', where the climate is temperate and lovely and the soil is rich. The rulers of Kashmir have loved and planted this valley like a vast garden from end to end. It is also grown in Italy, France, and Spain, from which countries more than three thousand pounds of saffron crocus are imported into the United States each year. The Spanish are particularly fond of its pungent flavour and rich colouring qualities for their paella and fancy sauces.

Gerard's description of the saffron crocus is excellent: 'The floure doth first rise out of the ground nakedly in September, and the long small grasse leaves shortly after the floure, never bearing floure and leafe at once. The which to express, I thought it convenient to set downe two figures before you, with this description, viz. The root is small, round, and bulbous. The floure consisteth of six small blew leaves tending to purple, having in the middle many small yellow strings or threds; among which are two, three, or more thicke chives of a fierie colour somewhat reddish, of a strong smell when they be dried, which doth stuffe and trouble the head. The first picture setteth forth the plant when it beareth floures, and the other expresseth nothing but leaves.'

To enjoy this classic beauty with its pleasantly bitter flavour, plant your corms in late spring or early summer and blooms will appear in October.

CAPERS
Capparis spinosa
of the Capparidaceae
family

Here are faithful companions that have been with us for a long time, and will be with us probably until eternity, for capers wear well. They have a wonderful aromatic flavour that comes from the unopened flower buds, just as in the case of cloves.

Capers are truly sensitive: the flowers open as the sun strikes and close as the sun sets, so the buds must be gathered very early in the morning between daybreak and sunrise. These flowers bloom on a prickly plant called the caperbush, which grows wild on the mountain slopes bordering the Mediterranean Sea, especially in Italy, Spain, and southern Greece.

The largest single use for capers is as a seasoning for sauces. These sauces usually accompany sea foods but they may be used succulently on meats as well.

CAPSICUM
Genus Capsicum
of the potato family

The Spanish call this spice *ají*. On Columbus' second visit to South America his ship's physician wrote in his journal that the

Indians ate a root called *ñame* (yam) and seasoned it with a spice called *ají* or capsicum

When one mentions capsicum, the word 'capsaicin' should be mentioned immediately, for this is the spice that creates the famous bouquet of the capsicums. Capsicum is a genus of South American and Asiatic annual subshrubbery plants of the potato family. Many species are cultivated for their fruits, which in some cases grow six to ten inches long. The fruits are fleshy, of many colours, and contain capsaicin, as do the seeds.

It is now time to point out that the capsicums are pepper plants but they have nothing to do with black or white pepper, used every day by almost everyone at every meal. Of all the peppers belonging to the genus Capsicum, it appeared logical to cover here only those that can be cultivated in almost every country in the world, and to cover pepper tabasco and the small red chili in Chapter 3. Actually, cayenne pepper is the only important and widely used pepper in the category just mentioned.

Of a very unusual nature, it has been called the purest and most certain stimulant. In times past it was used internally and externally as a local irritant. The health suggestion was, 'Take a hot bath every day, while in the bath drink a cup of capsicum tea, after the bath rub down with capsicum cayenne.'

Cayenne pepper has been called the most pungent of all spices. The good chef keeps cayenne at his finger tips as an indispensable flavouring for meats and gravies. Although it must be used with restraint, the right amount will add flavour interest to eggs, sauces, fish, and vegetables. It is an ingredient of pork sausage seasoning, and, of course, a part of curry powder. (See pages 128–131 for recipes.)

PAPRIKA
Capsicum annuum
of the potato family

The early explorers found *Capsicum annuum* growing in Central America. It was so attractive from all standpoints that they carried it back to southern Europe, where the plants flourished in Spain and Italy. They are also native to India and New Guinea. The capsicums were better known in an earlier day as ginny peppers. There are many varieties, and the fruits are called cods. Some cods grow upright, others hang down, some are extremely hot, others are mild and sweet. The colour range is from rich dark green to yellow and bright red. The paprika plant looks like a tomato or bell pepper plant with its fruit growing down. It is dearly loved for its mildness and rich colour. Like saffron, it was valued as a colouring agent.

We import large quantities of mild paprika from Spain; smaller amounts of a hotter variety come from Hungary and Yugoslavia. Paprika is also grown in California, where modern tunnel drying systems greatly speed the drying of the fruit. Europeans generally dry the fruit, or cods, in the sun.

There is scarcely a spice shelf anywhere that does not hold paprika, to use as a garnish or flavouring for many foods. Large quantities are used to give colour to meat products and in the preparation of condiments, catsup, and chili sauce. It is a part of the pepper mixture that is an important ingredient in curry powder. At America's drive-in eating places paprika has become a 'must' for the younger set's popular dish, french fried potatoes. The mild pleasant aroma and agreeably mild sweet taste, as well as the bright red colour, make the french fries flavourful and gives them zestful eye appeal.

It has been said that the use of paprika is valuable in maintaining good sight and that it helps to prevent night blindness. (See page 136 for recipe.)

9. *A time for pleasure and contentment*

Good health, good feeling, and a zest for living are ours for the asking. Along with restful sleep, eating is at the top of the list of things necessary to good health. Just eating, however, is not enough. Mealtime should be a time for real pleasure, a time for relaxation; a time for light and lilting conversation; a time for humour; a time for shedding our cares and worries; a time for ambitious contentment; a time to look forward to fragrance and flavour in the kitchen and at the table; a time to anticipate new taste thrills as satisfaction for the flavour buds on our palates.

Besides nourishing our bodies, a good meal nourishes the spirit and gives us the courage to deal with the many problems that are so much a part of modern living. A mundane meal is better than no meal at all, but very little better. To achieve inner satisfaction we must make use of spices and herbs. When used adroitly and with a flourish, spices and herbs can make the simplest food come 'alive'.

10. Spice chart: how the spices are used

PEPPER

GROUND: eggs: omelette, boiled, devilled, fried. Meats: beef roast, stew, steaks, chops, ground beef, lamb, veal or beef patties, turkey, duck, pheasant, pork. Sea food. Indispensable for meat sauces, gravies, and most vegetables.

CLOVES

WHOLE: baked ham, pot roast, hot tea, tomato soup, prunes, baked pears, beef tongue, pickles, cucumbers, peaches, tomatoes, and onions.
GROUND: pickle relish, fruit pies, a sprinkle on orange slices, chocolate drinks, and puddings, spice cakes, and cookies.

CINNAMON

WHOLE: pickled beets, cucumbers, peaches, pears, and crab apples; for flavouring hot chocolate and tea; simmer with fruit for compotes.
GROUND: french toast, fruit pies, sweet potatoes, baked custard, and in chocolate, lemon, butterscotch, banana, and lemon pies.

NUTMEG

Desserts: custards, eggnogs, muffins, cakes, pies, cookies. Vegetables: asparagus, cauliflower, lima beans, spinach. Meats: beef roast, chicken, stews. Lobster Newburg. Fruit: sliced bananas, fruit salad, rhubarb pie, apple pie. Hard sauce for plum pudding, also hot sauces for apple dumplings. Delicious when added to cream cheese on melba toast.

MACE

GROUND: pound cakes, chocolate pudding, most fruit pies. Vegetables: creamed potatoes, creamed turnips. Stuffing for chicken and turkey. Creamed soups, shrimp chowder. Fruits: superb with bing cherries, apricots, peaches, and pears. Good in jellies, salads, and biscuit doughs.

ALLSPICE

WHOLE: versatile for meat, vegetables, and dessert; beef, fish fillet, tongue, pork roast, roast duck, lemon slices for tea. GROUND: pickle relish; boiled shrimp; pot roast, gravy; beets; vanilla ice cream.

BAY

Dried bay very pungent; use sparingly. Swiss steak, beef, pot roast, stewed chicken and dumplings, lobster bisque, fish chowder, pork, soup, and sauces. Bay is included with spices because it must be bought where imported spices are sold.

GINGER

WHOLE or CANDIED: pear salad, dressing for fruit salad, cakes, and candies. GROUND: creamed chicken, fish sauces, roasts, shrimp curry, applesauce, squash (baked or creamed), cakes, and cookies. Sparingly over grilled cheese sandwiches. Wonderful in baked carrots.

CARDAMOM

WHOLE: candied as a confection, shaved on chocolate drinks, in fruits, salads, and sauces. GROUND: chicken curry, shrimp curry, hard sauces, fruit pies, Danish pastry, and demitasse coffee.

VANILLA

EXTRACT: ice cream, cakes, chocolate pie, sauces, custards, puddings, floating island, candies, hot chocolate, breakfast muffins, coconut pie, and eggnogs.

TURMERIC or CURRY	Curry is a blend of spices and herbs, mainly turmeric, cumin, and sage. GROUND: chicken, veal, fish, shrimp, liver, eggs, baked beans, French dressing, buttered cabbage, creamed onions, clam chowder, chicken salad, tuna salad, tomato bouillon, asparagus, fried eggplant, hash, and Swiss steak.
SAFFRON	Chicken curries, rice, bean soup, pudding, fish sauces, creole sauce, fish stuffings, lobster bisque, flavouring for cakes and pies, colouring for liqueurs.
CAPERS	Sea food salads, sauce for tomato and lettuce salads, canapés. Especially good with crab meat and lobster. Use this spicy little flower bud sparingly.
CAPSICUM	WHOLE: when pods are used in cookery they are called chilies. GROUND: RED DEVIL SQUASH CASSEROLE, fish fillets, scrambled or soft-cooked eggs, chicken fricassee, baked beans, corn, lamb or beef stew, vegetable soups, hamburgers, and SAVOURY PIES.
PAPRIKA	Creole sauce, creamed chipped beef, new potatoes, eggs, salads, veal, fried chicken, broiled fish, potato salad, salad dressings, garnishings. Paprika is a mixture of peppers but must be bought as a spice.

PART THREE

*Beverages and Seasonings
Other than Spices or Herbs*

11. Beverages

COFFEE
Coffea arabica

Water is the number one beverage in the world today. In second place is coffee, the background of which is as intriguing as that of the far-flung spices and herbs. According to legend, the flavourful wonders of coffee were discovered in the third century A.D. Monks fleeing from persecution found refuge in the highland of Abyssinia across the Red Sea. One night a father tending the flock ran to the monastery and cried, 'The animals are bewitched. They gambol and play as if it were a spring morn'. The prior tried to reassure him. He would go to the fold. He found that the monk was not seeing things. Night after night the animals continued to frisk about instead of sleeping as they should. The prior, after much study of the plants the animals browsed upon, was convinced that the sleeplessness was caused by the leaves and fruit of an unfamiliar shrub that grew in profusion there. He picked some of the ripe cherrylike fruit, chewed the seeds, felt exhilarated, and was very wakeful that night.

Whether or not legend is correct, Abyssinia and Arabia were the original homes of the coffee shrub. The Turkish ambassadors are said to have been responsible for the spread of coffee from Arabia to Constantinople, Venice, England, France, and other European countries. Coffee houses sprang up almost immediately and became popular with people of fashion, artists, and men of letters. The first coffee houses in England were established in 1652 and within twenty years were playing such an important part in the social and political life of the day that Charles II tried to suppress them on the grounds that they were 'seminaries of sedition'. Garroway's was one of the best-known coffee houses in England. Many coffee houses were also set up in Paris and became so important there that our common name for restaurant (café) is the French word for 'coffee' or 'coffee house'.

Until the seventeenth century all of the coffee of commerce came from Arabia. It was shipped from Mocha (or Mokha), once the capital of the province of Yemen. The name Mocha is still applied to all Arabian coffee as well as to other coffee resembling the Arabian in colour and taste. From Arabia, cultivation spread to Java in the Dutch East Indies and finally throughout the tropics of both hemispheres.

It is said that three-fourths of the world's coffee stems from a single tree. A few plants taken from the East Indies were presented to the King of France, who promptly sent them to the West Indies to be planted. This voyage was long and tempestuous and the plants gradually died one by one until only a single plant was left. Water became scarce but the faithful officer to whom the mission had been entrusted divided his tiny allowance with the plant, which lived to become the parent tree for the plantations of the New World.

The coffee plant thrives best in a fresh, dry atmosphere, where the temperature never goes below sixty degrees, and on land from eight hundred to five thousand feet above sea-level, where the soil is rich with red iron rust or with grey volcanic rock. The Brazilian state of São Paulo produces more coffee than any other place in the world. The other chief coffee-growing regions are Colombia, Venezuela, Central America, Mexico, Arabia, Africa, India, the East Indies, the West Indies, and the Pacific islands, especially Hawaii and the Philippines.

A fazenda or coffee orchard is a fascinating place to visit. As you approach, the wind sweeps out a great wave of fragrance like that of white honeysuckle, but sweeter by far. The shiny, dark foliage is covered with sparkling jasminelike flowers and it looks as though snow has just fallen. Gorgeous butterflies, bees, and locusts flutter and buzz all around while an endless number of hummingbirds dart about the trumpet-shaped flowers. The wild varieties of coffee grow as high as twenty feet but the cultivated ones are maintained at a level of six to ten feet so that the berries can be picked more easily. The berries are cherrylike and change from green to light yellow, then to scarlet, and last of all to a deep crimson or black. The skin shrivels when the berry is ripe and the pair of seeds found in most berries are covered with sweet yellow pulp. These seeds are the familiar coffee beans. Since the coffee tree often bears blossoms, green berries and ripe red berries at the same time, the berries must be picked by hand. No harvesting machine has ever been devised that could distinguish green from red!

In some berries there is only one seed. These are separated from the others because they bring a higher price in the market. The main blooming season in Brazil comes during the South American spring-time months of September, October, and November. It takes the berries six or seven months to mature, so the harvesters are busy from late April to early August. After depulping and many other compli-cated steps used in getting at the beans, they are packed in bags weigh-ing 132 pounds. Then they go to the seaports for distribution over the world. It is interesting to know that the flavour of coffee is improved if the raw beans are aged from one to four years before roasting. After roasting, however, they should be used as soon as possible since the delicate bouquet of roasted coffee deteriorates with age.

Practically everyone in Brazil drinks coffee, where it is made very thick and served in tiny cups for sipping. It is strong and invigorating. The United States buys approximately half of the world's coffee crop, as American consumption is the highest in the world; in proportion to population, however, consumption in the Scandinavian countries is slightly higher. Americans use the equivalent of 500 cups per person every year.

Coffee has been described as being the most versatile beverage in the world, and quite frankly I was amazed by this versatility as brought out through information very kindly furnished to me by the Pan-American Coffee Bureau. For instance, coffee is a rich source of niacin, an important B-complex vitamin. One well-brewed cup of coffee con-tains as much niacin as five slices of enriched bread. According to scientists, about half of the average daily requirement of niacin is found in five or six cups of coffee.

Further, if your family uses a pound of roasted coffee a week it is consuming the annual crop of about fifty-two coffee trees each year. About two thousand hand-picked berries are required to provide enough beans for a single pound of roasted coffee. This is slightly more than the annual crop of one average tree.

There are many ways in which to make and serve coffee before, during, and after a meal. But first let's look into the basic things to remember in preparing coffee, no matter what brand or type you use.

First, it is important that you buy the correct grind of coffee for your coffee maker. Try not to buy more than a week's supply at a time. Coffee exposed to the air for longer than that loses much of its flavour. Remember that the coffee pot itself must be very clean. Rinsing alone is not enough to remove the oils that collect on the sides each time it is used.

Once these pre-brewing details are taken care of, the actual brewing rules themselves are remarkably simple. Use enough coffee. You can't make good coffee if you skimp on the amount. The Pan-American Coffee Bureau recommends two level measuring tablespoons (or one standard measure) of coffee to each three-quarters of a measuring cup of fresh cold water for each serving. These same proportions apply no matter what type of coffee maker is used.

If you use a vacuum-type coffee maker or a percolator, timing is important. Percolator coffee should be 'perked' gently for six to eight minutes after it begins to show colour, and vacuum coffee must be kept over a low heat for not more than three minutes after the water has risen to the upper bowl. Drip coffee needs no timing, but if you stir the brew after it has dripped through you will get even strength throughout. And remember! Coffee must never, ever be allowed to boil!

In America we have relatively simple tastes in our favourite brew. No matter whom you asked how they like their coffee, the same answer would probably come from all of them and that would be, 'Make it fresh, make it strong, and make it hot'. But let's see how the rest of the world likes coffee.

In Arabia the average Arab drinks twenty-five to thirty cups a day, roasting his coffee beans at home and pounding them in a mortar. He boils water in a long-handled pot called an *ibrik*, tosses in the pulverized beans, and lets the brew foam up three times, removing it from the heat each time. He serves it in tiny, egg-shaped cups called *fin-djans*. In Armenia, Syria, and Turkey we find the same type of coffee, but with powdered sugar added to taste. In all these countries a pinch of saffron or cloves, or a few cardamom seeds, may be added before serving.

In Italy, coffee beans are roasted very dark, ground fine, and brewed, usually, in an espresso machine that uses live-steam pressure. The coffee is served strong and black with lots of sugar. A good Italian demitasse coffee can be made in small *machinettas*, available here, or in any drip or vacuum coffee maker, using two level measuring tablespoons of Italian-roast coffee to every three ounces of water. Sometimes a twist of lemon peel is added or a cinnamon stick is used to stir the coffee, giving it a slightly spicy flavour. This demitasse coffee is also the favoured drink in Latin-America.

Next we stop in Paris and Vienna. During the day the French people drink demitasse coffee similar to the Italian, but brewed in an ordinary French drip pot. For breakfast, though, our happy lot is *café au lait*, equal parts of fresh, strong coffee and hot milk, poured simultaneously. In Vienna they top their *café au lait* with a teaspoon of unsweetened whipped cream.

On page 152 are some proven recipes that will enable you to have fun with coffee.

There are hundreds of additional uses for coffee. For example, try it in desserts, in pies, in cakes and breads, candies and cookies, and in sauces and frostings. You will enjoy a new taste thrill when you enhance the bouquet of meats with coffee. Baste a leg of lamp sometime with a cup of coffee. Remember that the famous 'red gravy' of the South results from ham basted with black coffee. Also, try adding a little coffee to any meat gravy. There seems to be no end to the things you can do with coffee, a most unusual companion piece to the thread of life that never wears out—CONVERSATION!

TEA
Camellia thea

An old legend tells us that the wonders of tea were discovered by the emperor of China, Shen-Hung, quite by accident. Shen-Hung has always been thought of as the 'father' of Chinese medicine and agriculture. One morning he was boiling a pot of water near the woods (why an emperor should be boiling water this way is unknown) and leaves from an overhanging branch dropped into the pot. At the time his back was turned toward the fire, but he was aware of a fragrant smell under his nose. Turning in all directions and seeing the leaves in the boiling water, he traced the fragrance to it. Shen-Hung felt that any elixir that could do this, the likes of which he had never experienced, should be very flavourful. So he decided to sip the brew. Its bouquet was so appealing that he finally drank the entire contents of the pot. It was not long before he felt a new sensation—one of stimulation and vigour. The emperor immediately deleafed several branches from the overhanging tree, so that he could introduce this new wonder beverage to his court and later to his people. They shared the emperor's attachment to the new fragrance and flavour. This was the first step toward the expanded use of an exciting beverage that was destined to be associated with things pleasing and colourful.

The earliest reliable written record of tea is the *Ch'a Ching*, or *Tea Classic*, published in A.D. 780 by a scholarly circus clown named Lu Yu. He said, 'The best quality leaves must have creases like the leather boots of the tartar horseman, curls like the dewlap of a mighty bullock —unfolds like mist rising out of a ravine, gleams like a lake touched by a zephyr, and be wet and soft like fine earth swept by rain.'

Tea is indigenous to India and China, where it has been used for more than two thousand years. Some botanists say that it is a native of the entire monsoon area. China cultivates more tea than any other country and about one half goes for its own use. India is second in total cultivation but first in export volume. Japan and Formosa are other major sources for tea, and Ceylon, Sumatra, and Java also cultivate it as a major crop.

Tea plants will grow to a height of thirty feet if left untended, but for greater ease of picking, they are pruned and maintained at a height of three to five feet. The tea plant grows best at moderately high elevations in a warm moist climate. It reaches maturity in three years. During the blooming season there is a profusion of scented white or pinkish blossoms that look like little wild roses with petals circling a cluster of yellow hairlike stamens tipped with pollen. The leaves of the tea plant are leathery and lancet-shaped. They resemble the rose leaf and grow to a length of three inches. However, we never find them so long when we buy them because, during the picking, only the bud and three or four smaller leaves are harvested and none of these is over two inches in length.

When the tea plant reaches maturity it sends out an abundance of young leaf shoots and this is known as the 'flush' or the time for picking. As new shoots are grown on the twig, a new crop is picked. In Ceylon, Java, and Sumatra the climate is warm enough to bring about a 'flush' every ten days. In the colder parts of China, India, Japan, and Formosa new crops can be picked only three to five times each year.

Tea trade names don't come from the different tea plants but from the position of the leaf on the stem. The nearer the leaf is to the tip of the stem, the better it is in quality. Other determinants of quality are the height of the garden on the slope and care in cultivating and fertilizing plants.

The flavour of tea comes from the method of curing and the essential oils in the leaf. Its stimulating and refreshing qualities come from the small amount of theine, chemically the same as caffeine in coffee. It is an alkaloid and acts as a mild heart and brain stimulant. It could be dangerous if taken in excessive quantities. As a beverage, tea has the best fragrance and flavour when the leaves are steeped, never boiled, in hot water.

The processing of tea leaves is carried out in an exact manner wherever adequate equipment is available. First it is 'withered' outside for twenty-four hours. Then comes rolling, which consists of twisting or crushing slightly to bring the juices to the surface of the leaves. From here on the processing is slightly different for black tea and green tea. Black tea is fermented for four to five hours. Oxidation has then changed the leaves to a golden-brown colour and they have a pleasant aroma of ripe apples. Green tea is not fermented. (India and China prefer green tea while Britishers must have theirs black.) Between the extremes of black tea and green tea there are several kinds of teas that are submitted to varying degrees of fermentation. Among these is Oolong tea, only slightly fermented. It comes from Formosa and is the favourite of Americans. Next comes firing for half an hour. Hot air at a temperature of 220° F. is passed over and through the leaves.

Before tea is exported it is given a special firing and packed in lead-lined containers to keep out salt air, which would spoil the flavour. Tea absorbs odours most readily and it is sometimes scented in China and Formosa. Layers of jasmine flowers may be laid out on top of the tea for a few hours.

The Japanese, like the Chinese, prefer green tea. In Japan the drinking of tea has been elevated to such a pedestal that it now is taken with religious reverence. The tea ceremony is centuries old and is an institution in the cultural education of every Japanese of good family. Proper appreciation and proficiency take three years of study.

Coarse tea, steamed and pressed into bricks, is sent to Tibet and Mongolia, where it is used as currency. For the Tibetans and the Mongolians, tea is more than a beverage, it is a food. They add butter, soda, salt, and barley flour. They make this into a paste and call it *tsamba*, and they eat it as often as they can because it is such an unusual combination of fragrance and flavour. It is a staple in Tibet, as rice is in China and bread in Europe.

Turkestan likes fermented tea boiled until it is nearly black. Then cream and bread are added and it is eaten with a spoon. The Persians boil their tea and add spices of all known types. In Switzerland cinnamon is often steeped with tea leaves. The people of North Africa like an infusion of mint and tea.

Australians drink tea so strong that it tans the throat. The teapot is kept simmering on the fire all day. Australia's hobo, the swagman, carries a billy can in which he makes his tea. He carries it on his hip and calls it 'Matilda'. As the swagman walks, the Matilda seems to waltz around and around on his hip. 'Waltzing Matilda' has become a favourite Australian folk song.

The Russians like pressed brick tea. They sip the brew either from a saucer or from a tall glass similar to our ice cream soda glasses. They sweeten it heavily with a large lump of sugar and then add a piece of lemon for extra flavour.

The English drink five times as much tea as the Chinese, an average of about six cups per day per person. Fresh tap water, is boiled furiously, and the tea steeped for a full five minutes.

The leaves from a number of plants other than tea plants are used in making tea-like beverages. The most popular one is Paraguay tea, which is made from leaves taken from a holly-like tree in Brazil and Paraguay. American Indians also made a tea, called *yaupon*, from the leaves of a holly-like tree. It resembled strong black tea and was not unlike Oolong. *Yaupon* was widely used during Revolutionary times because of the very high taxes on regular tea. A tea is also prepared in Peru and Bolivia from dried leaves of the cacao tree. Trinidad tea is made from a decoction of the leaves of the pimento (or allspice) tree. It is used both as a beverage and as a medicine.

Beverages

Tea played an important role in our fight for freedom during the American Revolution. The Boston Tea Party, which took place on December 16, 1773, is remembered by everyone, but some of the reasons for it may have slipped temporarily from our memory. As the American colonists grew in stature and 'thinking' down through the years following the first settlement, it became apparent that there was a need for 'collective thinking and action' to protect the common interest, so the colonies were formed. Many years passed before they were able to stand up successfully for the things they believed in. Prior to the tea party the colonists gained confidence because of several successes with the British. In one case England was forced to repeal many objectionable measures. During that period such men as Patrick Henry and Samuel Adams were just waiting for a chance to crystallize the 'patriotic spirit'.

England obliged them by taxing tea and giving the East India Company a number of concessions, one of which was a monopoly on American trade. To prevent a consignment of taxed tea from being accepted in Boston, a group of indignant colonists had the famous tea party. These and other retaliatory measures were so drastic that they led directly to the rebellion of the American colonies.

American consumption of tea is lower now than at any time in the past, while coffee has reached an all-time high. Our 'taste in tea' is a simple one. We generally use one type and we like it either plain or with cream or sugar, with perhaps a hint of lemon. But there is a broad, exciting field just waiting for us to step into it. On pages 155 and 156 there are some hints and recipes that I hope will get you started on a new enjoyment of tea. See Beverage Chart on page 156.

COCOA
Theobroma cacao

Linnaeus, a famous botanist, gave cocoa the botanical name or *Theobroma cacao*, meaning 'food of the gods'. Not many other things on the earth can claim such an illustrious title. The hand of nature blends to perfection both the fragrance and the flavour that make up cocoa's bouquet right on the tree. Cocoa is the dried and powdered seed kernels of the cacao tree; as a beverage, it is more digestible than chocolate because part of the cocoa butter, or fat, contained in the beans is removed.

Cocoa first reached Europe from Mexico in the sixteenth century. It arrived about the same time as coffee and tea, and by the eighteenth century it had become popular throughout Europe. Cortez, conqueror of Mexico, was responsible for one of the first shipments to Europe. He demanded three hundred loads of cocoa from Montezuma, emperor of the Aztecs, as a part of the tribute to be paid.

Cocoa was looked upon with suspicion and uneasiness when it first entered the European picture. One superstition led to another. Europeans wanted to know just what this stranger from the West Indies was. Was it a food or a drink? Was it a nut or an invention of the devil? As soon as the superstitions were overcome, cocoa houses were established everywhere and with remarkable speed.

The cocoa tree grows to a height of ten to twenty feet, with long shiny, dark green and reddish leaves. The trunk of the tree is grey and white; the seed pods grow out of the trunk. When Friedrich von Humboldt first saw a cocoa tree, he wrote, 'Flowers were growing so low on the trunk as to be bursting through the roots right up out of the earth.' His delight was increased by the delicacy of the flower itself.

The tree is a *prima donna* among trees. It either flourishes or dies quickly and it is even necessary to have a nursemaid to provide just the right amount and type of shade. Seeds will not sprout unless they are planted within twenty-four to thirty-six hours after being picked. The tree reaches full development in the sixth year and will produce for as long as sixty years. The only successful large-scale plantations are located in Central America, the West Indies, and the South American and South Pacific areas.

There are many ways to prepare the 'food of the gods' but because of its very delicate and elegant flavour the method of preparation must be in the same vein. (See page 150 for recipes.)

12. Salt

Salt is a word of only four letters, yet these four letters have had a profound influence throughout the whole world! It is hard to imagine where civilization would be today without it. Salt has been used as a seasoning and preservative for food since time began. Bio-chemically, it is known as sodium chloride, but with the proper use of herbs and spices in cooking very little mineral seasoning such as this should be needed. All plants contain some salt in natural context with other essential minerals. The History of Salt is interesting to include here, but it is better avoided in diets which includes herbs by human beings and animals desirous of healthy living.

It is very plentiful on this earth but it is not evenly distributed. Where there was no supply near at hand, salt was brought from great distances. One of the oldest roads in Italy was called Via Salaria (Salt Road) because it was a salt transportation route. Salt made up much of the caravan trade in the Sahara Desert. Cursed by lack of salt, west and central Africa drew supplies from the open mines of Taoudéni in the desolate heart of the western Sahara, where it was quarried in tombstonelike blocks and reached Timbuktu and Goundam, four hundred miles to the south, by caravans of as many as six thousand camels. It is said that the French Sudanese reject any other salt, believing it lacks the curative properties of the desert product. Cakes of salt have been used as money in Tibet and the interior of Africa and it was so valuable in early times that our word for salary came from the Latin word *salarium*, which means 'salt money'. Roman soldiers were given an allowance to buy salt. This is the same common salt that we have on our tables at every meal and take so much for granted.

The world's most famous salt mines are located at Wieliczka, Poland. These mines were Poland's main source of wealth for centuries, but so much better salt is produced elsewhere that these once priceless mines have lost much of their importance in commerce. They are famous today as a show place and are illuminated by electric lights for visitors, who can ride a railroad down to a depth of a thousand feet. The mines form an underground city with sixty-five miles of 'galleries', on the walls of which miners have chiselled an endless array of fantastic figures. The figures depict a religious theme that was very often deliberate, but at other times accidental. There are holy images and two entire life-size chapels cut in salt.

Cardona is another famous name connected with salt. It is a small town in the northernmost part of Spain, close to the French border and not too far inland from the great eastern seaport of Barcelona. A huge dry ocean of extremely pure salt lies just three miles east of Cardona and there is not even the slightest trace of gravel or mould in it. From Cardona, salt goes to nearby small towns and to Barcelona and Tarragona, from whence it is distributed all over northern Europe and England. Numerous other salt beds are found in the surrounding lofty mountains. This mountain salt is the most unusual in the world. It is not white like other salt but is made up of all colours: rose, scarlet, blue, green, violet, yellow, and every shade of brown. When this beautifully coloured salt is pounded, however, every last vestige of colour disappears and it becomes snow white. Men have tried to preserve specimens but after a few years the colours fade and the salt crumbles.

The United States is the largest salt producer and the thickest beds are found on Avery Island just off the coast of Louisiana. America's very plentiful supply is one reason for her position in the industrial chemical field. Salt is the source of chlorine and sodium, two of the most basic building blocks in the world of chemistry. Only three per cent of salt production goes for human consumption. Salt has a use in the herb garden if only a destructive one. It is a safe weed killer when used in the hot weather. One pound to one gallon of water will kill the weeds quickly and if it kills weeds in such weak solution you will need no other argument to urge you to take herbs rather than salt as your flavouring.

13. Sugar

Saccharum
officinarum
From the
Arabic
Sukkar

Apparently the 'sweet tooth' has been with us always. In olden days fruits, which are chock-full of sugar, helped to satisfy mankind's desire for sweetness. The ancient Romans and Greeks had no sugar as such and used honey instead for sweetening. The busy bees were kept even busier to take care of the demand. This went on for centuries until man finally discovered a way to provide endless quantities of sugar by growing cane. Sugar was first produced in India as early as the first century of our era, either from bamboo or from sugar cane, but for many centuries it was used only as a medicine or as a rare delicacy at feasts. The Arabians, who gave Europe so many wonderful things, brought the sugar cane plant from India to the West and gave us its name. They introduced it first into the valley of the Tigris and the Euphrates, then into Egypt, and finally into Spain. It was not until the time of the Crusades, however, that sugar became generally known in Europe. The fourteenth century marks the earliest record of sugar in England and at that time it was used only as a medicine. The value of two pounds of it was equal to that of a pig or to as much as a carpenter could earn in ten days.

By the end of the fourteenth century Europe had developed a

flourishing trade in sugar, spices, and other products from the Orient by the overland route. Venice was the centre of this trade and maintained a monopoly until the fifteenth century, when a water route was found to India by Vasco da Gama. Gradually sugar cane reached the West Indies, Cuba, Mexico, and Brazil from Madeira and Hispaniola and the European nations were impelled to ensure an ample supply by reaching out for tropical and subtropical colonies. We all know the history of that era. Sugar cane was first grown in the United States in 1751 but it was of no great importance until seventy-five years later.

As a child, I remember walking with my father through the sorghum (*Sorghum vulgare*) fields on our farm in Virginia. He would break the tender stalks and taste the juice to test for flavour before cutting the cane for making molasses.

SUGAR
BEET
Beta vulgaris

The sugar beet now accounts for one third of the world's sugar production. The sugar beet comes from the temperate regions of Europe and America and first entered the picture at the beginning of the nineteenth century, at the time of the Napoleonic Wars. When the allies blockaded continental ports, Napoleon made large grants of land and money to encourage the sugar beet industry. The industry grew by leaps and bounds during the middle of the nineteenth century in Europe but did not become commercially important in America until the final decade of the century. Today, both the cane and the beet are very important crops in the U.S.A.

If you should happen to be a visitor in Amritsar, India, today you would be presented with a tiny cup of sugar and you would be expected to make a small present in return. The word 'candy' was taken from

Kandy, India, where a confection was made from sugar or molasses and combined with other substances to flavour, colour, or give the desired consistency.

You have very probably heard the saying that the only part of the pig lost by slaughterhouses is the squeal. With sugar cane, not even that much is lost. When the sugar is processed from the cane, a heavy molasses results and from this is obtained rum, alcohol, food for cattle, and fertilizer. The crushed stalks are also used as food for cattle and as fuel to run the mills, or it is made into fibre board for insulation. All that is actually lost is moisture, which returns to the atmosphere for a useful purpose.

It is sometimes said that we eat our weight in sugar every year and sugar consumption in a country is often referred to as an indication of its prosperity. This certainly must be true of America, since our sugar intake has increased right along with the growth in our standard of living. But what was said earlier about salt, applies equally to sugar. It is better taken in fruit than in isolated refined concentration.

14. Tussie Mussies

Our great-grandmothers carried tussie mussies when they had to sit in long religious meetings. The crushed scent helped when they felt faint. They also thought the aromatic, pungent aroma prevented infection. These quaint little nosegays were made up of several different flowers, mostly herbs. They were loved for their sweet-smelling oils and antiseptic virtues. The Southern debutante often carried them at coming-out parties, and the superstitious bride liked some of the sweet-smelling little flowers tucked in her old-fashioned wedding bouquet.

Take the tiny sweetheart rose for the centre and surround it with heliotrope, which in the language of flowers is 'Eternal Love and Devotion'. Marjoram comes next, for it means 'Joy and Happiness'. Violets, third, are the symbol of 'Modesty, Chastity, and Loyalty'. Sweet-smelling lavender comes next for 'Lovers True, and Strength of Heart'. Rosemary, the most significant herb of all, has been used since time immemorial for weddings. Rosemary is the sweet spicy herb for 'Remembrance'.

As the assembly with the delightful blessings of the gardens around the world comes to a close, I would like to remind the reader that gardening, the greatest of all hobbies, is waiting for you to pursue for a wonderful world of fragrance. The poem below, from an unknown writer, seems to have been written for the closing of this book.

Help us to plant and not destroy
The beauties others should enjoy.
Let us pass by and leave behind
A part of each, of every kind
Of scenery fair and birds in air,
Of fish in streams and blossoms fair,
So that ones who come our way
In some far distant day,
May say that we have guarded well
The treasures among which they dwell.

Acknowledgments

Inspiration and encouragement in the work that has gone into the writing and compiling of this book have come from many friends. The writer wishes to express her gratitude to all of them, in particular to those listed below:

My daughter Betty, Mrs Frank S. Doyle of Baltimore, Maryland, who helped so much in the home to make more time available to me for browsing, planting, and growing.

Frank B. Cox, Roanoke, Virginia, who lent me his cherished Gerard's *Herball* and acted as adviser and counsellor.

Raymond G. Rhodes, Kroger Company, Roanoke, Virginia, who located many of the hard-to-find spices and herbs.

James Jongerneel, Rye, New York, whose tremendous background of growing up in the Far Eastern countries and sitting on the Spice Exchange in London, was of much firsthand help.

Mrs John G. Berry, Garden Therapy Chairman—1954 National Council of State Garden Clubs, Goldthwaite, Texas.

Harold Lang, Roanoke, Virginia, a scholar and good friend.

Marie Johnston Fort, Griffin, Georgia, for her advice and encouragement.

T. C. Cheng, Washington, D.C., who told me of tea and the spices, especially ginger, and the curries of China.

Miss Emily and Miss Rory Cross, Richmond, Virginia, who shared flowering herbs from their Memory Garden.

Mrs Harry Brokaw Smith, American Herb Society, New York Unit.

Clarence S. Brigham, Director of American Antiquarian Society, Worcester, Massachusetts.

Marshall W. Neal, American Spice Trade Association, New York, New York.

F. Newman Turner, Editor of *Fitness*, Deanrow, Letchworth, Herts., England, for editing and adapting the book to English conditions.

L. G. Schermerhorn, Jr., W. Atlee Burpee Co., Philadelphia, Pennsylvania.

Acknowledgments

Wayside Gardens, Mentor, Ohio.

Breck's of Boston, Boston, Massachusetts.

Kennett E. Relyea, Farmer Seed and Nursery Company, Faribault, Minnesota.

Ellen Saltonstall, Pan-American Coffee Bureau, New York, New York.

R. H. Shumway, Rockford, Illinois.

Mittie Arnold and Margaret Thomas, Greene Herb Gardens, Greene, Rhode Island.

Albert S. Beecher, Associate Horticulturist, Virginia Polytechnic Institute, Blacksburg, Virginia.

Mrs J. W. Montgomery, Roanoke, Virginia, for her sincere interest and assistance in proof reading and editing.

Mrs John P. Kelly, Arlington, Virginia; Mrs Ted M. Jones, Bradenton, Florida; Mrs Henry Glasgow, Salem, Virginia; Mrs Edgar W. Smith, Akron, Ohio; Mrs John Carper, Salem, Virginia; Mrs W. W. Graves, Salem, Virginia; Mrs Tracy Lloyd, Roanoke, Virginia; Mrs Gordon Brooks, Roanoke, Virginia; Mrs Howard Creasy, Roanoke, Virginia; Mrs Ella M. Smith, Tampa, Florida; Mrs Fina Horner, Roanoke, Virginia; Mrs Charles Dawson, Salem, Virginia; Mrs Hazel K. Marshall, Roanoke, Virginia; Raymond Gene Kelso, Roanoke, Virginia; Mrs Henry Grady Moore, Washington, D.C.; Miss Eleanor M. Rankin, Washington, D.C.; Mrs Charles Farrelly, Roanoke, Virginia; Mrs Virginia P. Miller, Roanoke, Virginia; Miss Ellen Goodwin, Salem, Virginia; Mrs W. B. Adams, Roanoke, Virginia; LiliAnn Loubetta, Marseilles, France.

The various garden clubs who asked for programmes and kept me searching for legend, lore, and modern uses.

Betty Bond, WSLS Television, Roanoke, Virginia, who wanted her many viewers to share knowledge of our heritage of fragrance, flavour and beauty, and to be encouraged to plant and grow.

AND

Special thanks to my husband and son, who were my official critics, sounding board, and food tasters. They always showed joy and appreciation when a delightful aroma from the kitchen met them as they entered the house. The dishes were fragrant and flavourful, coming up totheir expectations, and they would beam with a happiness that is indescribable.

Bibliography

A book is a garden, an orchard,
a storehouse, a party,
a company by the way,
a counsellor, a multitude of counsellors.

H. W. BEECHER

A GARDEN, AN ORCHARD

Gerard's Herball 1597–1633
Brothers of the Spade
    Correspondence of Peter Collinson of London and John   1734–1746
    Custis of Williamsburg, Virginia . . . . . Swem   1948
Practical Floriculture . . . . Henderson   1889
Little Nature Library—Trees . . . . Rodgers   1917
Little Nature Library—Wild Flowers . . . . Blanchan   1923
Colonial Williamsburg: Its Buildings and Gardens . . . .
    . . . . Kocher and Dearstyne   1949
Taylor's Encyclopedia of Gardening   1936
The Years in My Garden . . . . Fox   1933
10,000 Garden Questions . . . .
    . . . . . . Rockwell, Free, Everett, Grayson   1933
Wild Flowers of America . . . . Rickett   1953
The Vine and Its Fruit . . . . Denman   1875
Garden Gossip
    Recording the Activities of Gardening in the Mid-South   1950–1958
Spices . . . American Spice Trade Association, Inc. .   1956
The Primer for Herb Growing. Herb Society of America .   1952–1954
Herbs, Their Culture and Uses . . . . . . Clarkson   1942
W. Atlee Burpee Co., Philadelphia (Catalogue)   1948–1959
Savoury Herbs Culture and Use . . . .
    . . . . U. S. Department of Agriculture
Greene Herb Gardens . . . . Greene, R.I.
R. H. Shumway, Rockford, Ill. (Catalogue) . . . . . .
Handbook on Herbs . . . . Brooklyn Botanic Gardens

Bibliography

A STOREHOUSE, A PARTY

The Medical Herbalist . . . . Yemm 1935–1937
The Historical and Scientific American Miscellany 1867
Choicest Productions of English Authors 1853
The World and Its People
    A Comprehensive Tour of All Lands 1934
Compton's Pictured Encyclopedia 1949
The National Geographic Magazines 1948–1959
Herbs for the Kitchen . . . . Mazza 1947
The Tasting Spoon . . . . Troup 1955
Culinary Herbs . . . . Kains 1920
Esquire's Handbook for Hosts 1949

A COMPANY BY THE WAY

The Old and New Testaments . . . .
Shakespeare Complete . . . . Irving 1943
Flowers from Old Gardens . . . . Trovillion 1951
Siftings, the Major Portions of the Clearing and Collected
    Writings . . . . Jen Jensen 1956
The Garden of the Bellflowers . . . . Baily 1953
The World in Your Garden . . . .
    . . . . National Geographic Society 1957
The Illustrated London News 1952

A COUNSELLOR, A MULTITUDE OF COUNSELLORS

WEBSTER'S ENCYCLOPEDIA DICTIONARY
    LIBRARY OF ESSENTIAL KNOWLEDGE . . . .
    . . . . Meine, Hopkins, Jr., Michaelis
    . . . . . . McDonal Leiper, Jr., Koffer, Graham 1943
THE AMERICAN COLLEGE DICTIONARY . . . .
    . . . . Barnhart 1949
EUROPE—A JOURNEY WITH PICTURES . . Fremantle, Holme 1954
Nature Encyclopedia of America . . . . Jordon 1956
Story of Nations . . . . . Rodgers, Adams, Brown 1955
Rand McNally World Guide . . . .
This Is America's Story . . . .
    . . . . . . Wilder, Ludlum, Brown, Anderson 1954
Hammond's World Atlas 1950

Bibliography

Webster's New Twentieth Century Dictionary . . . . .
. . . . McKechnie   1958
USEFUL QUOTATIONS—A CYCLOPEDIA OF QUOTATIONS .   1933
. . . . Edwards   1933

MAGAZINE

Fitness (and Health from Herbs). Monthly 1s. 6d. . . .
    Editor: F. Newman Turner, Deanrow, Letchworth, Herts

Index

Index

Thelma's clove pickle, 138
Theophrastus quoted, 82, 94, 99
Thyme, 110–11, 121; stuffing, 136
Trinidad tea (allspice leaves), 222
Tsamba (tea pastel), 222
Turmeric, 203–4, 212; dressing, 148;
garden salad, 147; industrial use of, 204
Turner, William, author of first English
Herbal, 11
Tussie-mussies (nosegays), 232–3

Universal mint sauce, 127
Upland cress, *see* Cress

Vanilla, 202–3, 211; icebox cake, 145
Venice, in spice trade, 185, 230
Vernage wine, 184
Vervain water, 76
Via Salaria, Italy, 226

Warton, on herb remedies, 184
Wassail bowl, allspice, 140

Water cress, 47
Watermelon rind pickle, 138
White ginger, 199
White mustard, 78–9
White pepper, 189; potato soup, 136
Wieliczka (Poland) salt mines, 227
Wild ginger, 121; spice, 200
Wild lemon, *see* Mandrake
Wild marjoram, *see* Pot marjoram
Wintergreen, 111–12, 121
Winter savory, 98
Witloof, *see* Chicory
Wood betony, 28–9
Woodruff, *see* Sweet woodruff
Wood sorrel, 103–4

Yam crisps, 149
Yarrow, 112–13, 121
Yaupon ('tea' of American Indians), 222
Yellow mustard, 78–9

Zanzibar spices, 85